Who Does She Think She Is?

The Heart-Centered Path to Professional Excellence

Wajhma Massoumi Aboud, M.D., MBA
Adriana Rosales, Founder of LATINAS100™

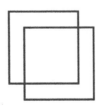

Las Vegas | New York | Mexico

Copyright © 2024 *Wajhma Massoumi Aboud*

Title: Who Does She Think She Is?
Subtitle: The Heart-Centered Path to Professional Excellence

ISBN: 978-1-959471-74-5 (Paperback)
ISBN: 978-1-959471-75-2 (e-Book)
ISBN: 978-1-959471-76-9 (Hardback)

Library of Congress Control Number: 2024927680

Cover design by RMPStudio™ Team
Edited by: RMPStudio™ Team
Printed in the United States of America
Las Vegas Nevada 89144

Publisher: RMPS, Rosales Mavericks Publishing Studio™, 1180 N. Town Center Suite #100, Las Vegas, Nevada 89144, www.Adriana.Company

No part of this book may be reproduced, stored in a retrieval system, or transmitted in any form or by any means—electronic, mechanical, photocopying, recording, scanning, or otherwise without the prior written permission of the author.

Limit of Liability/Disclaimer of Warranty:
The publisher and author have made every effort to ensure the accuracy and completeness of this book's contents. However, they do not guarantee that the contents are free from errors or omissions and disclaim any implied warranties of merchantability or fitness for a particular purpose. No warranty may be created or extended by sales representatives or written sales materials. The advice and strategies contained in this book may not be suitable for every situation. Professional consultation is recommended where appropriate. All events are loosely based on some real events and fictionalized characters.

The publisher and author shall not be responsible for any loss of profit or any other commercial damages, including but not limited to special, incidental, consequential, or other damages arising from the use of or inability to use this book.

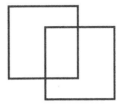

Dedication

To the women whose voices have been unheard and to those who feel driven by competition—may this book inspire you to rise above the noise, embrace your unique power, and come together. Let us replace rivalry with support, envy with encouragement, and build a future where
all women can thrive side by side.

Contents

Foreword	*7*
Introduction	*11*
Beyond Competition: Leading Together	*14*
A Story: Your Success, My Success.	*25*
The Heart of Women's Work: Leadership Energy	*34*
A Story: Leading with Compassion	*45*
The Four Pillars of Modern Leadership	*54*
A Story: Promises and Integrity go Hand in Hand	*65*
The Trickle-Down Effect	*71*
A Story: Turning Glances into Trust	*77*
Stress to Strength: Transforming Survival into Success	*87*
A Story: Man is Promoted Over Woman	*96*
Legacy Rising: Building the Next Generation	*101*
A Story of success: at what cost	*111*
Final Insights: Dr. Wajhma Massoumi Aboud	*121*
Final Insights: Adriana Rosales	*124*
A Call to Action	*128*
Afterword	*129*

Foreword

"Who does she think she is?" Those words, often whispered in boardrooms and punctuated in passive-aggressive emails, have echoed through the halls of leadership for generations. Intended to diminish, they have instead ignited a powerful call to action. When I first opened "***Who Does She Think She Is? The Heart-Centered Path to Professional Excellence***, I knew I wasn't just holding another book.

Leadership is not about titles, promotions, or corner offices. True leadership is about ***the courage to reimagine power***, to move it away from dominance and toward purpose. My own journey, from project manager to director to VP and eventually founder of Ascend & Transcend™, has shown me how the old, rigid paradigms of leadership are beginning to crumble, just not fast enough. This book doesn't merely acknowledge that shift; it accelerates it.

The brilliance of this work lies in its unapologetic premise: being heart-centered is not a liability. It is the superpower that unlocks next-level leadership and sustainable success. The authors dismantle the false dichotomy between respect and authenticity with precision and grace. Through relevant research, real-world case studies, and practical insights, they illustrate how emotional intelligence, empathy, and vulnerability, yes, ***vulnerability,*** strengthen teams, deliver exceptional results, and transform entire organizations.

What sets this book apart is its willingness to confront the uncomfortable truths about women in leadership, including the resistance that can come from other women. Rather than glossing over these complexities, the authors lean in, offering strategies to move from competition to collaboration, from suspicion to trust. They promote building authentic partnerships to shift how you approach mentorship, allyship, and peer relationships.

The chapter on boundaries struck a deep chord. As women, we are so often conditioned to overextend ourselves, to say yes to every request, to take on invisible workloads, to equate busyness with value. The authors boldly reframe boundary-setting as a strategic leadership practice, one that not only protects our well-being but elevates our impact. Their research underscores that leaders who master this skill cultivate innovative, psychologically safe environments where teams thrive.

As someone who earned my MBA and PMP while managing high-stakes projects and navigating corporate challenges, I understand the delicate balance between theory and practice. Transformation doesn't happen in lofty discussions; it happens in the reality of workday meetings, difficult conversations, and the daily choices we make about where to focus our energy. The authors get this. Their work provides insights needed to lead effectively in today's evolving professional landscape.

But what I treasure most about this book is its unshakable belief that excellence and empathy are not opposites; they are two sides of the same coin. As our world grows increasingly complex and interconnected, the future will belong to leaders who can marry analytical rigor with emotional intelligence and strategic thinking with human connection.

I encourage you to use this book as I have: to challenge your assumptions, sharpen your vision, and embrace your unique leadership signature.

And when you inevitably hear those familiar words, **Who does she think she is?** May this book remind you of the answer. You are exactly who you need to be: a leader who combines boldness with compassion, ambition with authenticity, and vision with heart. The real question is not who do you think you are? The real question is: Who will you become?

Amervis López Cobb, *MBA, PMP Keynote Speaker*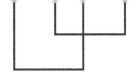
2X Best-Selling Author, Psychological Safety Expert, Founder, Ascend & Transcend™, and Author of Leading with Psychological Safety: 52 Essential Practices for a Year of Building Trust and Empowering Teams

Introduction

As the co-authors of "Who Does She Think She Is? The Heart-Centered Path to Professional Excellence," we are honored to invite you on a transformative journey through the tapestry of human experiences that shape organizational success based on our personal experiences and deep insights.

Adriana and I come from diverse backgrounds. I, Dr. Wajhma Massoumi Aboud, have spent over 18 years navigating the complexities of healthcare finance and administration. At the same time, Adriana's expertise spans military service in space command, telecommunications, entrepreneurship, and the world of publishing. Yet, despite our distinct professional paths, we are united by a shared belief: *the most impactful leaders are not those who climb the corporate ladder through ruthless competition but those who cultivate environments where everyone can thrive and feel seen and heard.* When we discuss competition in the subsequent chapters, it does not refer to the capitalist social framework of competition but the competition among peers and colleagues in the corporate space. Behind corporate walls, where competition can be detrimental to the goals of the company mission and detrimental to those ruthlessly competing for resources or perceived titles within the organization.

Through a blend of captivating storytelling and strategic insights, we have woven a narrative that transcends the traditional boundaries of business literature. This is not merely a guide and blueprint to career advancement and organizational optimization; it is a clarion call for a fundamental shift in how we approach leadership and corporate culture. At the heart of this work lies a profound truth: ***the greatest success is not measured by titles or accolades*** but by the legacies we leave behind, the lives we touch, the communities we uplift, and the positive change we inspire. From Adriana's own journey navigating the complexities of the telecommunications industry to my transformative work in healthcare, these pages offer a roadmap for building organizations that prioritize human connection, foster trust, and unlock the full potential of every employee.

As you immerse yourself in these stories, prepare to be inspired, challenged, and ultimately empowered to redefine the very nature of corporate leadership. We invite you to embrace a new paradigm where ***empathy, integrity, and compassion*** take center stage. This is a call to action, a rallying cry for a new generation of ***heart-centered leaders*** who understand that the greatest impact comes not from personal ambition but from a steadfast dedication to uplifting, supporting, and empowering those around them. Staying true to our book title, "Who Does She Think She Is?" we intend to discuss the dynamics between women leaders who have helped us better understand why our unique female voices might

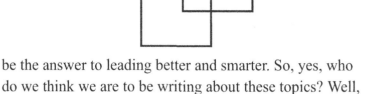

be the answer to leading better and smarter. So, yes, who do we think we are to be writing about these topics? Well, we've been there, done that, and then some!

Together, we have the power to transform corporate cultures, reshape the business landscape, and leave a permanent mark on the world. *So, let us embark on this journey, guided by the wisdom of our shared experiences and the unwavering belief that the future of leadership belongs to those who <u>dare to lead with their hearts.</u>*

Wajhma Massoumi Aboud, M.D., MBA
Adriana Rosales, Founder of LATINAS100™

Beyond Competition: Leading Together

As a woman in the corporate world, I've often found myself more competitive than the average male alpha and even more so than most women I've collaborated with, or at least that's how it's felt. Growing up as a young Latina in a small agricultural town in the Bay Area, California, I learned early on that survival required more than just resilience; it demanded a relentless drive and an attitude of overcoming the stigmas placed upon me by societal norms. Coming from a background of poverty as a child of Mexican immigrants, I knew I had nothing to lose because I quite literally had nothing to begin with. Of course, that shifted for me in my early twenties when I entered the corporate space after my military career.

While working in corporate America, I looked around the corporate boardrooms; for the most part, I was the only woman. This sobering reality remains all too common, with women still making up only 29% of C-suite

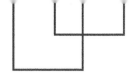

positions and Mid-entry roles leading to C-suite roles. Even more startling, I was a rarity because women of color represent only 7% and Latino women holding just 1.4% of C-suite positions, making them the most underrepresented group of these roles, while white women account for 22%. (LeanIN, n.d.) Unlike most, I realized I had an opportunity to change more than just my circumstances. By extending my hand to other women, I could help shift that statistic and pave the way for broader representation, proving that collaboration, not competition, is the key to rewriting the narrative for women in leadership. This revelation was the first step in transforming my path and the corporate landscape.

One thing I learned early on growing up in a Latino family was that the ideologies people hold about how the world should work are very different from how the world actually works. In a Latino household, the cultural ideology centers on collaboration, not competition. It's the collective efforts of the family that keep everyone afloat in a country that systemically marginalizes Latinos. This is not the typical American way of life, where self-reliance and individualism are often celebrated.

Many Americans are fond of saying, "Pull yourself up by your bootstraps," but that's a difficult task for those who don't even have boots, let alone shoes. For people like me and millions of other Americans, thriving in a society focused on productivity where your work often equals your value means relying on your community and embracing collaboration, not competition. These early lessons in the power of unity would later profoundly shape my approach to leadership.

The competition ideology seemed foreign to me as a child. Being competitive was not something I was used to experiencing growing up. However, growing up in the United States taught me quickly that I had to be smarter, faster, and tougher than those who didn't share my background, and competition was a way of surviving and navigating the American ecosystems. This meant that pursuing a career in the arts or music wasn't realistic, and I was conditioned to believe I needed a "real job." That belief was ingrained deeply in my youth, primarily because I was taught to compete for resources and the mere sake of competition as a revered American sport, not by my family but by the American school system. We need to look no further than how we test and grade our children in our current school system. Competition as an ideology and capitalism as a fundamental idea are very American ways of navigating life; often, people confuse them to be the same, but they are quite different ways of operating in the world. But that's a story for another book. Suffice it to say, my upbringing instilled in me a unique perspective on the interplay between competition and collaboration - one that would later inform my leadership philosophy and ideology.

So, what does all of this have to do with competition versus collaboration? The truth is that collaboration, not competition, is the key to lasting success both personally and professionally, especially in corporate spaces. The data is clear: collaboration is more effective in driving profits, enhancing workplace morale, and delivering better outcomes for employees and shareholders. As someone who has fiercely competed in corporate America, I can confidently say that companies prioritizing collaboration over cutthroat competition consistently perform better. I know this to be true because, as a corporate executive in telecommunications for many years, hiring thousands of people, leading, and training them, I saw firsthand how collaboration always prevailed. These experiences solidified my belief in the transformative power of collaborative leadership.

Early in my corporate career, after serving in the United States Air Force, I worked for a prestigious marketing firm in Silicon Valley. There, I learned one of the most valuable business lessons: working more hours doesn't necessarily translate into better results. It's often the opposite. The key lies in working smarter, not harder. This principle is why those who seem "lazy" are sometimes the smartest. They find efficient ways to achieve goals without burning themselves out. As a society, we often forget that humans are not machines and that we can get more done through collaboration. You could say it's the lazy way of doing work, but data shows it is the most effective way of living, and nature self-validates this. We thrive in environments that nurture collaboration, creativity, and organic growth. This insight would become a cornerstone of my leadership approach, shaping how I built and managed teams.

To add a broader perspective on competition, it's worth referencing Charles Darwin. Darwin is often misunderstood as promoting "survival of the fittest" in a purely competitive sense, but his observations were more nuanced. In The Descent of Man, Darwin states: "In the long history of humankind (and animal kind, too), those who learned to collaborate and improvise most effectively have prevailed." (MedTRADE, n.d.) This quote highlights that collaboration, not just competition, is fundamental to survival and success. While competition has its place, Darwin recognized that cooperation is equally, if not more, crucial for thriving in complex environments. This insight aligns with reality in nature and business: those who succeed long-term often learn how to work together, leverage collective strengths, and build alliances. This is why so many Latino families and others with similar cultural backgrounds can triumph and succeed in environments foreign to their customs; they rely on collaboration to help one another rise regardless of their circumstances and disadvantages. Darwin's observations resonated deeply with my experiences and bolstered my commitment to fostering collaborative environments.

Alfie Kohn further supports this notion in his book No Contest: The Case Against Competition. Kohn's research dismantles the myth that competition is inherently beneficial, showing that collaboration fosters stronger relationships, greater innovation, and better results in nearly every area of life. Kohn writes, "The assumption that competition is natural and desirable is so ingrained that we seldom stop questioning it. But the evidence shows that cooperation, not competition, leads to better outcomes." (JournalAntiTrust, n.d.) Kohn's work provided an evidence-based framework for the principles I had intuited throughout my life and career, reinforcing my dedication to collaboration as a leadership tool.

Understanding the power of collaboration is essential in a world where women are often pitted against one another. True, the corporate world is still competitive by nature, but the real advantage for women lies in cohesion and mutual support. As we navigate our careers, we must strive to lift one another, knowing that our collective success far outweighs any individual victory. This is the ethos I aimed to embody as I climbed the corporate

ladder, always seeking to empower and uplift my fellow women leaders.

Looking back at my journey from a small agricultural town in California to navigating corporate boardrooms, I see the tension between competition and collaboration not as mutually exclusive forces but as complementary dynamics. Growing up as a young Mexican American girl, I believed in the American dream. I was taught that hard work, determination, and competition were the paths to success. (by my teacher, not my parents) And to some extent, that's true; competition has its place. But the truth is that it's collaboration that amplifies success. When women come together and share our experiences, knowledge, and support, we create a force that competition alone can't match. This is the power we must harness to transform the face of corporate leadership truly.

Like many others who have risen above prejudice and poverty, my story proves that while competition drives individual progress, collaboration builds lasting change. In corporate spaces, where women often fight to be heard and seen, embracing harmony and mutual support is our most significant advantage. Yes, I'm competitive. But more than that, I believe in the power of sisterhood, and I've learned that success is far sweeter when shared. As women striving to leave their mark on the world, we must remember that while competition can fuel our ambition, collaboration propels us forward together. Through this lens, we can begin redefining leadership and reshaping corporate culture.

In Who Does She Think She Is? The Heart-Centered Path To Professional Excellence, we'll continue to explore how embracing collaboration as a core value can unlock doors that competition alone cannot. By supporting each other, we not only enhance our success but redefine what it means to lead in a world that often underestimates the power of unity and women uniting through female solidarity. For a long time, while I was still in the corporate space working as an executive in sales and training hundreds of women and men, the undertone of "Who does she think she is?" was the background music. On many occasions, I felt that most women defaulted to this question and engaged with other women similarly. I

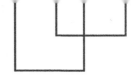

hope to answer this question as we explore these chapters and topics together. Who do I think I am? The answer lies in the collective journey we will undertake as we challenge assumptions, share insights, and rewrite the rules of corporate leadership and how women interact in corporate spaces.

Three Key Takeaways for Enhancing Collaboration in the Corporate Setting:

1. Build Trust by Sharing Knowledge and Resources
In competitive environments, people often withhold information to gain an edge. Break this cycle by openly sharing knowledge and resources with your colleagues. Building trust through collaboration establishes a foundation of mutual support and creates an environment where everyone can succeed. **This is the bedrock of a genuinely collaborative culture.**

2. Mentorship and Peer Support Networks
Create or join a mentorship program or peer support network where women can share insights, experiences, and strategies for navigating corporate challenges.

Empowering others through mentorship strengthens the bonds of solidarity and ensures that collective wisdom is accessible to everyone. Lifting as we climb creates a rising tide that benefits us all.

3. Celebrate Collective Wins, Not Just Individual Achievements

Shift the focus from individual accomplishments to team successes. When you achieve a goal, highlight how collaboration made it possible. Recognize and celebrate the contributions of everyone involved, reinforcing the idea that working together is more powerful than competing against each other. By reframing success as a shared endeavor, we foster a culture of unity and mutual support. (Yes, I know, depending on your industry, of course!)

These actionable steps can transform corporate culture, fostering a work environment where collaboration truly outshines competition. As we embark on this journey together, let us remember that our strength lies in our ability to unite, empower one another, and lead with compassion and solidarity. *Through this lens, we will redefine what it means to be a woman in the corporate world and, in doing so, create a brighter future for us all.*

A Story: Your Success, My Success.

" She doesn't have the qualifications." I looked at her in confusion. I wasn't sure where she was going with this. One of my colleagues, Diana, continued complaining that the new Interim Vice President, Monica, did not have the qualifications to apply for the Senior Vice President role. She did not understand why Monica was up for promotion. In my mind, I didn't agree. Monica was brilliant, witty, and hard-working. She had experience in the field for at least a decade. She certainly had the education, with two Master's degrees. She was bright, and everyone who worked with her loved her. Yet, I did not understand why Diana opposed Monica getting the promotion. Was it because Monica was younger yet brighter than her? Diana continued, "I just don't think she has the professional maturity." I wasn't sure that was true, but I nodded yes. I left as I had a meeting, but the thought bothered me all day long. The next day, when I went to work, I brought it up with another colleague, Anisha. I told her that Monica would be great for the Senior Vice President position. She smiled and said, "Are you kidding me? She is only being considered because the CFO has a thing for her." I replied to her with confusion, "Are you sure? I don't think so. I do think she's qualified and should be given a chance." Anisha smirked and said that she could interview all she wanted and that it was too late. I did not understand, so I asked her to explain. She said, "A group of us met with the Board yesterday, and we threatened to step down from our positions if they considered her candidacy." I was saddened to hear this. This particular candidate was lovely. Monica was fantastic and would have done so well in that role. She worked so hard, was talented, and brought in more profits than anyone else in our district, yet these women, her closest colleagues, did not think she was qualified. They also went as far as to sabotage her chances of getting a job. What would it take? What more did she need to do to prove that she was qualified? The CFO and all other leadership wanted to hire her for the role of Senior Vice President, yet her own "trusted" peers, some of whom had trained her, held her back.

These women were upset and felt so threatened by this woman who clearly had all the qualifications for the job. Yet, they collectively did not want her to be in that position. The only explanation is that they were jealous.

She was talented and beautiful. Do you remember the L'Oreal commercial in the 1980s where a beautiful model says, "Don't hate me because I'm beautiful!" I truly believe these women hated this woman because besides having the highest credentials, experience, and a great personality, she was also very beautiful. What did they care if Monica would be successful or not? What difference would it make to them? Why did they see her as a threat? None of them really knew her. All they saw was this very friendly, bright, and beautiful red-headed woman who always smiled. She was like fire though. Monica always had the best answers and ideas. I would be excited to go to any meeting she attended, mainly because I knew that in that session, I would learn something. She was always willing to share her knowledge and helped me and others whenever she could. So then, what was the problem? Why was this position so impossible that this young, vibrant, highly educated woman could not do it? One of the other VPs once mentioned that it is unfair that she would be considered because she is so young and doesn't have the experience she had. She said I have been in my position for the past twenty-five years. How is she going to get a higher position than me? I trained her, after all. I was stunned at this reaction. So, I asked her if she applied for the position. Her exact words were, "No, I don't want the responsibility." Then why weren't these women helping each other? Why did they not want to help Monica rise to the top and shine? She certainly had the ambition and smarts. Yet, they looked at her as if she had applied to a job that should only be offered to a rocket scientist. Monica's promotion would certainly not take anything away from any of them. Their salaries would remain the same, and they certainly had the same opportunity to apply for the same position. So what was the problem? Is our innate human jealousy so intense that it prevents us from helping others? And why does it matter if someone else shoots for a goal that you did not even take a shot at?

Monica was a star in every way. I have noticed the power of women. As cliche as it may sound, we can be so strong together. It particularly hurts when women use their power for counterproductive actions. In this instance, I sincerely felt that they became mafia-like over the wrong reasons. Can you imagine if they brought that same mafia-like power to the table and helped Monica instead? One thing I know is that people generally like and feel good about helping people. If these women came together and helped Monica succeed, they would have much more fulfillment and satisfaction in their hearts. More than my own successes, I have found so much joy and pride in my heart when someone I have trained rises to the top. Had these women helped Monica instead, their own lives would have had a positive effect. Rather than bittered with negative thoughts, they would bloom with positive thoughts, knowing they helped someone walk towards their dreams.

I was on my way out of the office and going shopping at a nearby sample sale, and I walked Monica to the elevator. As always, she looked very well put together and was wearing a beautiful black and white suit, which made her hair look more red than usual. Being almost six feet tall, I looked down at her and noticed how tired she looked, and it was only the middle of the day. She looked like life beat her up. She looked like she was at war and not winning. I knew she must have received notice that she would not be invited to attend the next interview rounds. Rejection can be heavy on the heart and body. She looked at me, and tears started to pour down her cheeks. She was hurt and sad. I let her know that I was on my way to a sample sale and that she should come with me. She nodded yes! as I didn't think she wanted to be at work any longer that day. We walked silently through Fifth Avenue, and we both understood that what just happened to her was unfair and unjust. After some serious retail therapy, Monica was laughing again. We walked to the subway station; she hugged me and thanked me. We both knew that wouldn't be the end of her career.

Soon after receiving the rejection notice, Monica left and was appointed President of a similar organization. Clearly, she had the education, work ethic, and talents. Wouldn't it have been wonderful if those women held together firm and helped her grow in areas where they felt she was lacking? It would have been wonderful to support this woman who had what it took. The organization lost one of its most significant assets. As I suspected, I later found out that many were jealous of Monica because she was beautiful and bright. Having those two qualities seems to be a massive threat to women. I have heard from many that if a woman is brilliant, she is not very pretty. And if she is beautiful, then she probably does not have the smarts for the more prominent roles. We would all live in a much better place if we put those biases aside. And to understand that beauty is truly skin deep. Beauty lies within. And like we teach our children, it doesn't matter how good-looking someone is or isn't; we must respect and treat others as we would like to be treated. All of that aside, think about how it would have been had these women collaborated with Monica to integrate solidarity to help each other elevate their careers, perhaps into different departments or other companies. Instead, these women chose to break down a human being instead of empowering one. This is a prime example of how competition and jealousy hurt companies and employees.

Three takeaways for enhancing collaboration instead of competition and jealousy:

1. **Cultivate a Success Abundance Mindset**

   - Recognize that another's success doesn't diminish your achievements
   - Transform competitive energy into collaborative power by celebrating peer accomplishments
   - Build a culture where victories are shared, not hoarded

- **Key Action:** Create regular forums to spotlight team members' achievements, making success a shared experience rather than a zero-sum game.

2. Champion Growth Through Mentorship

- Convert experienced knowledge into lifting power for emerging leaders
- Transform expertise from a protective shield into a bridge for others' advancement
- Recognize that nurturing others' growth enriches the entire organizational ecosystem
  - **Key Action:** Establish cross-generational mentoring relationships where seasoned professionals actively guide rising talent, creating a legacy of shared success.

3. Lead with Heart-Centered Recognition

- Look beyond surface judgments to recognize authentic talent and potential
- Challenge unconscious biases that limit perceptions of leadership capability

- Foster an environment where diverse strengths are valued and amplified
    - **Key Action:** Implement objective performance metrics while creating space for highlighting unique contributions that transcend traditional measures of success.

Remember: True organizational strength comes not from individual stars shining alone but from a constellation of leaders illuminating the path forward together.

These takeaways reflect the heart of transformative leadership: when we lift others, we all rise higher.

The Heart of Women's Work: Leadership Energy

It goes without saying that women, with all our beautiful nuances and incredible talents, have divergent leadership styles compared to most, if not all, men. In fact, the first time I realized that working with women was different from working with men was when I entered the civilian world after my military career.

My naïve attitude about leadership styles between men and women was quite a distorted ideal. For me, the military was one of adventure and travel, primarily with male colleagues. More often than not, I only worked with men, and those interactions seemed seamless, effortless, and downright fun and natural. My career was such that collaborating with women was seldom, and because of the nature of my work and duty station, isolation was a common theme. Noticing that women were few and far between wasn't something I thought about. It was the 90s, so I figured that this was just the way things were and that every career would be like this. Teamwork and collaboration were a military theme. In fact, those of us

with military backgrounds pride ourselves on what we can build and accomplish through collaboration. This was very familiar to me because of my cultural background. The ideology in Latino culture is collective, not self-reliant, like the culture in the United States outside of the military. The military felt like home to me because everyone had the same mission and vision within their unit. In the military, we weren't lone lions hunting alone but rather a pack of wolves working together to devour our prey. I know this sounds extreme and quite visual, but you get my point: teamwork was the master controller, not for individual profit but for the collective greater good. In my case, while in the military, the goal was to protect our country and do it while jumping out of planes, delivering goods, and deploying resources with our big jumbo aircraft to other countries in the name of peace and diplomacy. Just to be clear, I personally never jumped out of planes, but some of my colleagues did, and that was as close as I wanted to get.

Many years later, after my military career, I found, after much research and polymath behavior, that it's not really about male or female leadership styles but rather feminine or masculine energies, meaning the emotions certain individuals emote while exhibiting more feminine or masculine traits as they lead. This became deeply important to me because after I transitioned out of my military career into the corporate world, I continued to expect the reciprocity of teamwork and collaboration, but what I found was disconnection, discontent, and people fighting over rank and resources while violating every ethical and moral human code for the sake of bottom-line company profits and larger employee bonuses at the expense of one's very soul. In a nutshell, what I found behind every corporate environment was people stepping over others to get to the top without an iota of remorse. This is not to say that military culture was perfect or any better, but it was different in the sense that adherence to a strict and ethical moral compass is monitored and rewarded.

Now, as it pertains to how women work in the workplace, well, I know two things for sure. One is that women have a vastly different level of understanding of the world than men do, and this matters because we must understand ourselves first in order to understand others. How did I come to know and understand these things?

Well, because I speak on stage often and discuss the topic of leadership, you can imagine how many books I've read on the subject. One of my favorites on the subject of leadership and how men and women lead differently is by Dr. Pauline Crawford, The Power of Authentic Harmony: Magical Conversations Transforming Our World. I first met Dr. Pauline over five years ago and found her work to be quite interesting as it pertains to gender dynamics. In her book, Dr. Pauline explains how some women have more masculine energies, and some men have more feminine energies. At first, I was a bit perplexed because I had never heard about these concepts. However, she explains it this way:

Dr. Pauline Crawford's model of authentic harmony revolves around understanding and aligning various communication and personality styles to create more meaningful and transformative interactions. Central to her model are four archetypes: the Ruler, the Philosopher, the Magician, and the Sovereign. Each of these archetypes represents a distinct approach to communication, leadership, and collaboration, providing individuals with a framework to better understand themselves and others in both personal and professional contexts. The key point here is that this is simply a "Framework" that can help anyone in the workplace better understand the dynamics between women and men.

- *The Ruler archetype* is characterized by a love for action and a focus on solutions. People who align with this archetype are often seen as natural leaders, driven by results and motivated by the need to take charge in conversations and decisions. Rulers thrive in environments where they can make things happen and direct outcomes. They focus on problem-solving and efficient action, often prioritizing tangible results over emotional or relational considerations.

- *The Philosopher archetype* is driven by a love for people and seeks synergy in relationships. Philosophers are deeply connected to the human aspect of interactions, valuing empathy, understanding, and the alignment of ideas. They aim to foster cooperation and harmony

among individuals, serving as the glue that holds teams and relationships together.

- *The Magician archetype* is centered around ideas and collaboration. Those who embody the Magician archetype are creative thinkers who excel in environments that encourage innovation and brainstorming. They enjoy collaborating with others to generate fresh ideas and solutions, thriving on the excitement of possibility.

- *The Sovereign archetype* prioritizes feelings and community. Sovereigns are deeply connected to their emotional intelligence and are driven by a desire to foster strong, supportive relationships. They focus on creating a sense of belonging and unity, often stepping into roles that emphasize care and support for others.

Dr. Crawford's model encourages individuals to reflect on their archetype preferences and their gender dynamics that will allow recognizing the strengths and potential blind spots that each style brings to conversations. By understanding their own tendencies, individuals can also become more attuned to the communication styles of others, fostering deeper connections and greater mutual understanding. This model is particularly valuable in personal and professional settings, where communication and collaboration are keys to success.

Had I known this framework earlier, I would have approached things differently in the corporate world. I would have understood that women operate differently than men in the sense that some women lead from the Magician archetype (Masculine energy). In contrast, others lead from a Sovereign archetype (feminine energy). Men also vary in leadership types. For example, men sometimes lead from the Ruler archetype (Masculine energy), and some men lead from the Philosopher archetype (Feminine energy). This distinction makes a difference. Understanding how women work in the workplace is of the utmost importance because it affects how we do business and how we do life. In the following chapters, I will explore how this understanding is crucial to the "trickle-down effect. More to come on this topic. For now, let me link all of these ideas together and share a few tools with you.

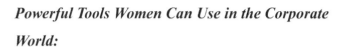

Powerful Tools Women Can Use in the Corporate World:

Foster Authentic Harmony: Embrace Dr. Pauline Crawford's framework of Ruler, Philosopher, Magician, and Sovereign better to understand your leadership style and those of others. Recognize that collaboration thrives when people embrace their unique archetypes.

Leverage Feminine and Masculine Energies: Acknowledge that both masculine and feminine energies have value. Understand your natural inclination and how to balance these energies to be an effective leader.

Build Networks Through Magical Conversations: Engage in conversations that are open, authentic, and inclusive. Create spaces where you and your colleagues can express diverse perspectives and work towards shared goals.

Focus on Emotional Intelligence: Cultivate emotional awareness and sensitivity. This will not only enhance your leadership but also strengthen team bonds and foster a positive work environment.

Practice Empathy and Collaboration. Foster environments that prioritize collective success over individual gain. Encourage teamwork and create an atmosphere where everyone feels valued.

Promote Inclusivity: Ensure that all voices are heard and that different leadership styles and energies are respected. Inclusivity builds stronger teams and drives innovation.

By implementing these tools, women can lead more effectively, contribute to a healthier work environment, and build stronger, more valuable networks. Think about it for a second: what style have you been operating under? What has your "energy" been like at work? Do you bring in more of a "rule with an iron fist" type of leadership style or an "all is well" leadership style? Can you recognize any of the archetype traits in yourself?

In this chapter, I share my journey from military service to corporate leadership, revealing a profound truth about leadership energy that transformed my understanding of workplace dynamics. Through my transition from the structured, collaborative military environment to the competitive corporate world, I discovered that effective leadership isn't simply about gender it's about the delicate balance of feminine and masculine energies that each of us carries.

Drawing from Dr. Pauline Crawford's groundbreaking framework of the four archetypes Ruler, Philosopher, Magician, and Sovereign, I learned that these energies shape how we lead, communicate, and build relationships in the workplace. This revelation helped me understand why some of us naturally gravitate toward action-oriented leadership while others excel at fostering community and connection.

What fascinates me most is how this understanding bridges the gap between military-style collaboration and corporate competition. When we recognize and honor these different leadership energies, we create spaces where both individual excellence and collective success can thrive. Instead of forcing ourselves into traditional leadership molds, we can leverage our natural inclinations while appreciating the diverse strengths others bring to the table.

The tools I've shared here aren't just theoretical, they're practical approaches I've seen transform workplace dynamics. By embracing authentic harmony and building networks through meaningful conversations, we can create organizations that value both results and relationships, both strategy and soul.

Looking ahead to our discussion of the trickle-down effect, remember: your leadership energy creates ripples that touch every corner of your organization. The question isn't whether you're leading with masculine or feminine energy, it's whether you're leading with awareness, authenticity, and purpose.

This is the heart of women's work in leadership, not mimicking traditional power structures, but reimagining them through the lens of our unique strengths and experiences.

A Story: Leading with Compassion

I couldn't believe the words coming out of my mouth. I couldn't believe I was asking for help, but I was desperate. Have you ever found yourself in a work situation where circumstances are dire, through no fault of your own, and you need someone to help rescue you? Wouldn't it be a dream come true if we all had that safety circle at our workplaces? A circle of trust? This is a story about ensuring compassion and empathy at work because, in life, you never know when that person needing empathy and compassion could be you or someone close to you.

My heart ached as I asked her to help me save my job and professional reputation. We were on the phone, and all I heard on the other side of the line was silence, followed by a sigh. "I am so sorry; I will not be able to help. I have already set plans with my staff, and I will not be able to adjust now," she said. I was shocked by her response. Just four weeks earlier, I had run into Asha, who had promised to help me and seemed genuinely sympathetic to my situation. She had assured me that she had openings in her department and would love to hire me. For her to completely change her tone was disheartening. She lied and made up an excuse. It was just that, an excuse. It wasn't that she couldn't help me; it was that she didn't want to. Asha was interested in helping herself by staying out of workplace politics, *even if it meant not doing the right thing.*

A few weeks earlier, I had asked Asha to go on a walk with me. During our conversation, I explained my current difficulties with my boss, Wendy, whom Asha was not fond of. She mentioned hearing some rumors but wanted to know the full story. She seemed so sincere and kind that I opened up to her, believing she truly cared and would help if needed. I explained the situation about my boss, who was known throughout the organization for being verbally abusive. It was common knowledge that if any employee disagreed with her, she would find a way to terminate their employment.

When I first started working there, I couldn't believe such a situation could exist. However, as time progressed, I witnessed the horror of working in an abusive

environment. I no longer felt psychologically safe. From the day I disagreed with how she handled a client situation; I began to notice plots forming against me. First came the humiliation at board meetings, then what felt like deliberate setups over minor matters. When her name appeared in my inbox, my heart would race, my palms would sweat, and breathing became difficult. Yet I had no choice but to endure. As the only child and primary breadwinner for my household, I desperately needed this job. Additionally, I had recently developed health issues and needed to maintain my insurance coverage.

During my recent annual checkup, my gynecologist found something concerning and performed a biopsy. The diagnosis was Stage 1 cancer. Though I had no symptoms, I needed insurance for the upcoming treatments. As if the timing couldn't be worse, my mother was also ill, and I was helping to care for her. My father had passed away the previous year, leaving me responsible for supporting both myself and my mother.

Despite these personal challenges, my work performance never wavered. Every project was polished, and my work quality remained exceptional. I maintained a professional appearance and confident demeanor; no one suspected my struggles. To others, my life appeared perfect. I hadn't shared my conflicts with my boss with anyone until that moment with Asha.

The empathy in her eyes made me feel vulnerable as I shared my experiences. My reputation at work was stellar. I was considered a role model for the office, consistently receiving exceptional performance ratings and evaluations. I dealt with my difficulties by immersing myself in work. When I shared my story with Asha, I believed she would help me escape this abusive situation. My intention wasn't to manipulate her; in fact, with my years of experience, exceptional leadership skills, and interpersonal abilities, she would have been fortunate to have me on her team. However, the toxic work environment had eroded my self-esteem, making it increasingly difficult to maintain this perspective.

As conditions at work became increasingly hostile, I approached Human Resources, but they dismissed my concerns. I began searching for other positions, though my options were limited. Time was running out as my cancer treatments were approaching. I couldn't manage both chemotherapy and a toxic work environment while supporting my mother. On that snowy winter afternoon,

Asha faced a choice: she could open or close a door of opportunity. While she didn't owe me anything personally, she had often spoken about women supporting each other and promoting female advancement. Despite my challenging circumstances, I had earned an Executive of the Year Award through peer nomination and led the most efficient and organized department with exemplary processes.

Though the situation with my boss was complex and difficult to explain, it demanded understanding and compassion. I knew that if our roles were reversed, I would have done everything possible to help someone in desperate need. When I make a promise to help someone, I honor that commitment. While disappointed, I've learned that life's challenges make us stronger. I often wonder how different our professional world would be if women consistently supported each other, helping one another build cultures that promoted these values. The strength and success that could emerge from such solidarity would be remarkable.

When Asha chose to look the other way, I learned a valuable lesson: not all leaders possess the strength and skill we expect of them. Some people prefer to observe drama rather than help those in need. This experience prompted me to reflect deeply on the kind of life I wanted and the culture I wished to be part of. Ironically, I hadn't needed to ask Asha for a favor given my experience and expertise, having me on her team would have benefited her. Shortly afterward, another executive within our organization sought me out. I continued to excel, completed my chemotherapy, and have remained cancer-free for the past decade.

After surviving cancer, I committed to living more purposefully. I founded my own company, cultivating the culture I had always envisioned. Partnering with seven other strong women, we've built a thriving business. Not all women turn away in times of need, and my current circle of friends proves this. These women are strong leaders, friends, and mentors who don't just listen to problems but actively help devise solutions.

Imagine working in an environment surrounded by powerful, intelligent, beautiful women who genuinely want to help. Picture facing a workplace challenge and having a group of colleagues who listen to your concerns and collaborate on solutions. This is precisely the culture we've created in my company. We lift each other up

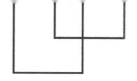

rather than tear each other down. We don't turn our backs on employees; instead, we recognize and retain talent. We acknowledge the sacrifices our team members make and support them without getting entangled in unnecessary politics. We take pride in leading with compassion and integrity.

Imagine such a workplace for a moment. Doesn't it inspire you to work harder and achieve more?

Three Key Takeaways for Crisis-Tested Leadership:

1. The Courage of Conscious Choice

• Every leadership moment presents a choice between self-preservation and moral courage

• Crisis reveals the gap between proclaimed values and actual behaviors

• True character emerges when helping others carries personal risk

Implementation Tool: Create an "Ethics in Action" handbook that guides difficult decisions during high-pressure situations, including clear protocols for supporting team members in crisis.

2. From Personal Crisis to Organizational Vision

• Individual challenges can become blueprints for systemic change

• Professional excellence and personal struggles often coexist Like Sir, Richard Branson says "I don't think of work as work and play as play. It's all living."

• Tomorrow's leaders are shaped by today's responses to adversity

Implementation Tool: Develop "Phoenix Programs" that help employees transform difficult experiences into leadership opportunities and organizational improvements.

3. Building Resilient Safety Networks

• Strong organizations need both formal and informal support systems

• Crisis intervention requires both immediate action and long-term support

Implementation Tool: Establish "Resilience Circles" - cross-departmental support networks that provide both professional advocacy and personal support during challenging transitions.

Practical Application Framework:

- Institute "No-Questions-Asked" transfer policies for toxic reporting relationships

- Create confidential advocacy channels separate from traditional HR

- Develop leadership metrics that measure both performance and compassionate action

- Build emergency response protocols for personal/professional crises

The Four Pillars of Modern Leadership

As someone who has navigated both military and corporate landscapes, I've witnessed leadership through multiple lenses. Now, as an entrepreneur, I continue evolving as a servant leader, guided by professional coaches, mentors, and countless leadership resources. But here's what's fascinating: the intersection of traditional leadership qualities with the unique strengths women bring to leadership creates something extraordinary. Let's start with the foundational leadership qualities but view them through the lens of feminine leadership power:

Self-Awareness:
This isn't just about understanding your strengths and weaknesses; it's about embracing your authentic self in leadership. For women leaders, self-awareness intertwines with Dr. Pauline Crawford's concept of authentic harmony. Whether men or women embody more of the Ruler, Philosopher, Magician, or Sovereign

archetype, understanding your natural energy and how it impacts others becomes your leadership superpower.

Integrity:

In a world where women often face additional scrutiny, integrity becomes more than just ethical behavior; it's about consistency between values and actions. This alignment is crucial for building trust, particularly in corporate spaces where women are still breaking through traditional barriers. Like the collaborative spirit I learned in my Latino household, integrity in leadership means staying true to your values while lifting others up and bringing your authentic you to work with integrity.

Vision:

Great leaders don't just see the future, they create it. For women leaders, vision often includes seeing beyond traditional competitive models to embrace collaborative success. Drawing from my military experience, where teamwork transcended individual achievement, I've learned that the most powerful visions are those that unite and elevate entire teams.

Communication:
Here's where women often shine brightest not just in traditional communication but in what I call "The Connector" role. As John Maxwell wisely noted, "Everyone communicates, but few connect." Women's natural ability to forge deep connections transforms essential communication into something far more powerful: ***authentic relationship building.*** (women's superpower)

Beyond these traditional qualities, I've identified four additional traits that define exceptional leadership, particularly for women:

1. Foresight Leadership: The ability to anticipate and prepare for future challenges while creating opportunities for collective success.

2. Compassionate Leadership: Leading with strength and empathy, understanding that these aren't mutually exclusive but mutually reinforcing.

3. Courageous Leadership: The willingness to challenge traditional paradigms and create new paths forward, especially in spaces where women's leadership styles haven't traditionally been celebrated.

4. ***The Connector vs. The Communicator***: Moving beyond mere information exchange to create meaningful bonds that strengthen teams and drive results.

These traits become especially powerful when viewed through the lens of collaboration rather than competition. As I detail in my book "Corporate Code: A Bottom-Up Perspective on Great Leadership," women possess a unique ability to transform traditional leadership paradigms through connection, collaboration, and authentic presence.

This transformative approach to leadership isn't just about individual success it's about creating a trickle-down effect that changes organizational cultures and inspires future generations of women leaders. When we lead authentically and embrace our natural strengths as connectors and collaborators, we don't just achieve our own goals. We create pathways for others to follow.

The magic happens when we stop trying to fit into traditional leadership molds and instead embrace our unique qualities as women leaders. Whether you're naturally more aligned with masculine or feminine energy, the key is authenticity combined with intentional connection. This is how we shift the paradigm of shallow and weak leadership altogether.

Remember: the best leadership isn't about mimicking others or following prescribed rules. It's about leveraging your authentic self, embracing your natural abilities as a connector, and creating environments where collaboration trumps competition. That's where true leadership excellence begins and where women often lead the way.

However, my journey to understanding these leadership qualities and particularly how they manifest differently for women has been deeply personal. During my early corporate career as a young executive in my twenties and early thirties, I fell into a common trap: believing that survival in the corporate world meant emulating masculine leadership styles. Fresh from my military career, where I had primarily worked with men, I adopted

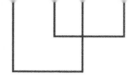

their rough-around-the-edges attitude, thinking it was the only path to success.

This mindset was a product of my environment and experience, but it wasn't sustainable or authentic. It wasn't until my early forties, after years of intensive personal development, leadership training, and mentorship, that I had an epiphany: I didn't need to lead like a man. In fact, embracing my authentic feminine leadership style has proven far more effective for my professional success and personal well-being.

This transformation didn't happen overnight. It came through deliberate investment in my growth through books, coaching, private conferences, and mastermind groups. As Warren Buffett wisely advocates, "The best investment you can make is in yourself." This investment isn't just financial; it's an investment of time, effort, and willingness to evolve.

Through this journey, I discovered what many forward-thinking leaders now acknowledge: the era of ruling with an iron fist is over. Today's most effective leadership embraces traditionally feminine qualities, empathy, connection, and collaboration qualities that women often naturally possess. This isn't just my observation; I've encountered countless male leaders who now recognize that these "feminine" leadership traits usually produce superior results.

This realization led me to develop my perspective on leadership, which I share in my book "Corporate Code: A Bottom-Up Perspective on Great Leadership." Beyond the traditional leadership qualities mentioned above, I've identified four additional traits that genuinely define outstanding leadership, especially for women who want to lead authentically rather than trying to fit into traditionally masculine leadership molds. Here they are as I wrote them in my book but a story:

Picture this: It's 2001, and I'm sitting in my first corporate office, my perfectly pressed suit feeling like armor against a world I barely understand. The transition from military precision to corporate politics wasn't just challenging; it was triggering. Every unexpected email notification, every veiled office threat, and every competitive sidelong glance sent my hypervigilance into overdrive. The PTSD symptoms I'd been managing since

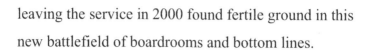

leaving the service in 2000 found fertile ground in this new battlefield of boardrooms and bottom lines.

One particular Wednesday morning stands out. After another sleepless night of replaying workplace conflicts, I found myself hiding in a bathroom stall, trying to steady my breathing while my colleagues attended the weekly strategy meeting. My military training had taught me to be strong, to push through, to never show weakness. But this wasn't combat, this was corporate America, and somehow it felt even more dangerous to my nervous system. The breaking point came during a high-stakes presentation. As I stood before the executive team, a senior VP's aggressive questioning style triggered a full-blown panic attack. At that moment, frozen before my peers, I realized something profound: the toxic leadership styles I was witnessing weren't just damaging to company culture; they were literally making people sick.

This realization became the foundation of my leadership philosophy and the four pillars that would transform my approach to leadership. Through Foresight Leadership, I learned to anticipate and create psychologically safe spaces before crisis emerged. Compassionate Leadership taught me that acknowledging vulnerability both in ourselves and others creates stronger, more resilient teams. Courageous Leadership meant challenging toxic behaviors even when they were uncomfortable. And most importantly, the Connector principle showed me that true communication goes beyond words to create genuine human bonds. Our organizations deserve leaders who understand that power flows from creating environments where everyone can bring their whole selves to work. When we lead from this place of authentic strength, we don't just transform businesses, we heal workplaces, empower individuals, and create lasting positive change.

This isn't just theory. Its wisdom was earned through battles fought not just in military service but in the trenches of corporate America. And it's the foundation for building organizations where both people and profits can flourish together.

✔ *Trust:* This goes beyond basic reliability. It's about creating an environment of "outrageous trust" where people feel empowered to bring their authentic selves to work. As I learned from my experiences in Silicon

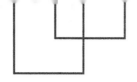

Valley, when leaders demonstrate deep trust in their teams, people rise to exceed expectations. This isn't just about trusting others; it starts with trusting yourself and your instincts as a leader.

✔ *Courage:* The courage to lead differently, challenge outdated paradigms, and stand up for what's right even when it's difficult. Courage isn't just about being brave; it's about having the courage to be vulnerable, admit mistakes, and create spaces where others feel safe to do the same. As I learned in my military career, true courage often means taking responsibility first.

✔ *Compassion:* In today's rapidly changing business environment, compassionate leadership isn't just lovely to have; it's essential for success. This means understanding that every employee is a whole person with hopes, dreams, and challenges. My experience in Puerto Rico taught me that the most potent leadership moments sometimes come from showing patience and understanding while people grow into their potential.

✔ ***Connection:*** As mentioned above, great leaders must master the art of genuine connection beyond mere communication. As John Maxwell wisely noted, "Everyone communicates, but few connect." This ability to forge authentic relationships to truly see and understand others transforms good leaders into great ones. It's about creating an environment where people feel heard and deeply understood.

Remember: The best leadership isn't found in books or taught in seminars. It emerges from the daily practice of these principles, from staying true to your values while helping others achieve their full potential. That's where true leadership excellence begins, and that's how *we'll transform the future of business, one heart-centered leader at a time.*

A Story: Promises and Integrity go Hand in Hand

Excitement filled the air as we gathered to celebrate. Samantha had worked tirelessly to reach this milestone, and the offer letter seemed a mere formality. Her interviews with the C-suite had been exceptional, with unanimous enthusiasm for her joining their leadership team. A true mathematical virtuoso, Samantha brought more than just technical expertise she brought passion. You could find her at her desk late into the evening, meticulously reviewing spreadsheets. She added pivot tables and typed out perfect formulas, making sure every number had a purpose. Her attention to detail was legendary; she wouldn't rest until even the smallest discrepancy was resolved.

Hand-picked from Harvard's prestigious MBA program, Samantha embodied everything our company sought in a future partner and president. Her brilliant mind was matched by her generous spirit – she regularly took time to mentor others, including me, breaking down complex business decisions into clear, data-driven insights. "It's all

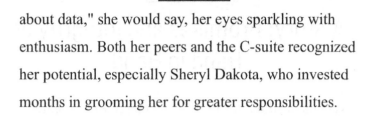

about data," she would say, her eyes sparkling with enthusiasm. Both her peers and the C-suite recognized her potential, especially Sheryl Dakota, who invested months in grooming her for greater responsibilities.

One crisp morning, as sunlight painted the city in golden hues, Samantha and I met at our usual spot, the metro station five blocks from the office. The spring in her step matched the optimism in her smile. "It's a great day," she shouted, radiating confidence. During our walk, she shared her meticulously crafted 90-day plan, each element thoughtfully designed to elevate the organization. This promotion wasn't just deserved; it was the natural progression of her remarkable professional journey.

Sheryl Dakota had been Samantha's strongest advocate, holding considerable influence within the organization. She had consistently championed Samantha's candidacy, even sharing the committee's unanimous support.

The shift came unexpectedly during an all-hands meeting, one week before the official announcement for the Chief Financial Officer of Global Affairs position. Mr. Hollis, a senior executive from another department, entered quietly and requested to speak with Sheryl Dakota, the Selection Committee Chair. From my seat beside Samantha, I watched Sheryl's expression transform from warm assurance to guarded concern. Her repeated glances in our direction spoke volumes, even as she nodded and murmured, "I understand."

After Sheryl's conversation with Mr. Hollis, something fundamentally changed. While Sheryl maintained her professional smile, in the coming days, she noticeably distanced herself from discussions about the position.

The morning of the announcement, anticipation hung heavily in the air. I arrived early, obsessively refreshing my inbox. When the email finally appeared "ANNOUNCEMENT: New Chief Financial Officer" my hands trembled as I read the unexpected news: Sandy Williams, a relatively new hire, had been selected as Chief Financial Officer of the Global Affairs Department.

The phone felt heavy in my hand as I dialed Samantha's extension. "Sandy Williams?" I blurted out," The same

Sandy who struggles with Excel and relies on a handheld calculator for basic P&Ls? Who couldn't complete her Master's in Sociology?" A quiet sniff on the other end of the line preceded Samantha's request to meet on the rooftop.

Twenty minutes later, I found her there, tissue box in hand, tears flowing freely. The truth emerged: Mr. Hollis had leveraged his influence to recommend Sandy Williams, owing to a favor for another department's CEO. Rather than advocate for the most qualified candidate, Sheryl had chosen political expediency over principled leadership. The rationale offered – that Sandy was "a better fit" – rang hollow against Samantha's stellar qualifications and proven track record.

The aftermath revealed the true cost of compromised integrity. Perhaps Sheryl feared for her own position, or maybe she thought supporting Samantha might limit her future advancement. Whatever the reason, her choice to prioritize politics over merit undermined the organization's foundation of trust and excellence.

Predictably, another company soon recognized Samantha's exceptional talents. Today, she ranks among the most successful leaders in her industry, a testament to the truth that while organizational politics may win the moment, true merit ultimately prevails.

Three Essential Takeaways for Leadership Integrity:

1. Honor Your Commitments
- Leadership credibility hinges on following through
- Trust, once broken, creates lasting organizational damage
- Courage in upholding promises defines true leadership character

2. Choose Merit Over Politics
- Short-term political gains often result in long-term cultural losses
- Excellence should transcend personal favors and political convenience
- Strong organizations prioritize capability over connectivity

3. Build Cultures of Trust
- Leadership decisions create ripple effects throughout organizations
- Supporting excellence attracts and retains top talent
- Integrity in leadership breeds integrity in culture

Remember: Our promises shape not just individual careers but entire organizational cultures. When we choose courage over convenience, we build institutions where excellence naturally thrives.

The Trickle-Down Effect

During a pivotal moment at John Maxwell's Leadership Conference in Orlando, I experienced a profound shift in my understanding of leadership and what it actually means to lead. It was the mid-2000s, and I was deeply immersed in my corporate executive role, overseeing vast teams across multiple financial institutions. My days were filled with the complex choreography of managing hundreds of employees, orchestrating thousands of new hires, and developing high-performing sales teams. Yet even as I poured my energy into building stronger organizations and more effective salespeople, I recognized that my own growth journey was far from complete.

At this particular conference, I encountered several high-level executives who recommended Kevin Kruse's "Employee Engagement 2.0," (KevinKruse, n.d.) where he explores the "spillover effect" or "trickle-down effect." The concept resonated deeply with my experience both as a leader and a mother. Here is why: each morning, as I rushed my teenage son to school, I would resort to yelling and bribing him with PlayStation privileges to get him out of bed. If I couldn't effectively communicate the value of education to my own child, how could I inspire my employees to invest in their personal development? Kruse's work revealed a profound truth: a leader's state of mind and energy level biologically and physically trickles down to their entire team. This revelation sparked intense self-awareness. I had spent nearly 90% of my corporate career in a state of stress. As a single woman with a small child who married in my late 30s and had another child during my marriage, I could shoulder more responsibilities than most because for the better part of my life, I was not married and had no children. While this resilience served me well in climbing the corporate ladder, it came at a significant cost.

The implications were utterly blatant. By sending my son to school in a state of anxiety because of my yelling and coercing him to comply with PlayStation privileges caused his elevated cortisol levels before school, I was setting him up for failure. He couldn't possibly engage effectively with learning in that physiological state.

Similarly, when I arrived at work carrying the residual stress from my morning battles, that energy transferred directly to my team. This understanding connects directly to John Maxwell's "Law of the Lid" principle: employees can only grow to the level of their leader's capacity. If leaders don't understand the fundamentals of human physiology, stress management, and self-regulation, they inadvertently create a ceiling for their entire team's potential. The solution lies in becoming students of ourselves and understanding our bodies, minds, and psychological patterns. As the ancient Greeks wisely advised, "Know thyself." This isn't just philosophical wisdom; it's a practical imperative for modern leadership. We must learn to regulate our own stress responses before we can effectively lead others.

This trickle-down effect ripples through families, communities, and generations. When leaders operate from a place of stress and anxiety, that energy cascades through their organizations and into their employees' homes. Conversely, when leaders prioritize well-being and emotional regulation, they create environments where both people and performance flourish.

My deep understanding of this reality led me to become a certified HeartMath® Coach, helping me understand this trickle-down effect at a scientific level. The transformation in my leadership style yielded immediate results, both at home and in the office. Here's what happened with my son:

One morning, instead of our usual chaotic rush, I took a moment to center myself before waking him. I sat on his bed, placed my hand on his shoulder, and spoke quietly about the opportunities awaiting him at school, especially that young girl in his history class whom he really liked. No bribes, no threats, just authentic connection. That day marked the beginning of a profound shift. Over the next few months, his grades improved, but more importantly, his attitude toward learning transformed. School was no longer something he was forced to do but something he wanted to participate in. Why? Well, here's the science: he could reason and respond without his fight or flight response, making him hate what he was being forced to do. Today, as a successful military service member, he often reflects on that period, noting how my emotional regulation helped him discover his own potential for growth. He still thinks that I overdo the calm and

collective bit, but hey, it works. He is now on track to become a parachute rigger in the Army. I'm so proud of him.

The lesson is clear: leadership energy creates ripples that touch every life we encounter. When you step through those corporate doors, your state of mind affects your entire organization. As leaders, we must recognize that our teams constantly observe, assess, and mirror our behaviors, both consciously and unconsciously.

Here are three crucial insights for energy-conscious leadership:

1. Mind Your Entry: Before entering any space, assess your energy and emotional state

2. Monitor Your Delivery: Pause and regulate before engaging if you're not in an optimal state

3. Embrace Heart-Centered Leadership: Lead with empathy, connection, and authentic presence

The future belongs to leaders who understand that their energy and presence directly impact team performance and well-being. When we lead from a place of regulated energy and genuine service, we create environments where both people and profits naturally thrive.

Remember: Your state of mind isn't just your personal matter; it's your first act of leadership each day.

A Story: Turning Glances into Trust

My heart raced as I pressed the blue button labeled "Launch Meeting." The screen opened, and I saw my reflection smiling back at the camera. Only two people had logged in. I remained muted, watching as attendees filled the screen, then a second screen, and finally a third. The CEO introduced me as the new Vice President of Corporate Communications. As he shared my work history with the department, I maintained my smile while nodding, yet I couldn't help but notice several women in the meeting texting each other. Smirks were exchanged, and eyes rolled reactions that, unfortunately, were all too familiar in corporate environments. The unfriendly stares and hostile glances continued as the CEO detailed my professional achievements.

I made an effort to ignore the negative energy, focusing instead on my sick baby. Jenny had been up all night with a fever, and it had taken everything in me to prepare for my first day. Every muscle ached from three sleepless nights, yet my desire for this new opportunity burned bright. That morning, I managed to care for Jenny, clean the house, and prepare breakfast for the four-year-old twins. The house needed to be spotless since my critical mother-in-law would watch the baby during my meeting. After four exhausting days of tending to my sick child without a moment for self-care, I finally washed and styled my hair to perfection. The finishing touch was the Christian Dior lip gloss my husband had given me for Mother's Day.

As I prepared, I repeated my daily affirmation in the mirror: "I was born to do this job, and I will not give up until I am successful." Deep in thought about the previous night's challenges, I noticed the CEO had stopped speaking and turned the floor over to me. Silent claps flickered across Zoom screens while I ignored the women's sidelong glances. Their lack of interest in my success didn't matter. I had finally reached a place where I could feel proud of my achievements.

I began speaking, only to see five chat messages appear and several people pointing to their ears, mouthing "you're muted." Quickly unmuting myself, I expressed my excitement about the opportunity. The Zoom room, filled with mainly female middle managers and directors, offered not one genuine smile or nod, only perfunctory congratulations flowing through the chat.

The meeting continued with my boss announcing housekeeping items and plans for an in-person welcome celebration that Thursday during anchor day. Despite my excitement to begin working with my team of six women, I harbored a naive hope that they weren't among those exchanging cold glances during the video call. I had always believed that higher positions would bring more collaboration and teamwork among colleagues, but experience had taught me otherwise.

As the Zoom squares began closing with casual waves goodbye, I rushed to check on Jenny. Her fever persisted, and she had apparently vomited twice during my meeting. My mother-in-law's whispered commentary didn't help: "I don't understand how a child can get sick during summer." She continued reminding me that her children never fell ill during summer months. After enduring three hours of criticism about the house's cleanliness, the children's eating habits, and my husband's appearance, her departure brought immense relief.

I focused on preparing for Thursday, my first official day in the beautiful high-rise I had admired while dropping off my children at school. The thought of sharing my vision and expertise within those walls energized me. Each night, I tended to Jenny, watching her slowly improve.

Thursday morning arrived after just two hours of sleep. At 4 AM, I stood in the quiet living room, gazing at the silent city. Even the lights seemed tired. Looking up at the clear, crisp sky, I silently prayed for strength. Despite my credentials and experience, I worried about the reception awaiting me. The baby's cry interrupted my reflection, but this time, with good news, her fever had broken. "Thank you, God," I whispered. My husband took the baby, assuring me he would handle both her and the twins. Before reaching the door, my husband called out, "You look really pretty, tone it down a little. Remember what happened last time." I smiled but felt the weight of those words. How could I forget the attacks

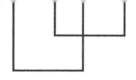

from women in my previous organization? The lies spread behind my back, the character assassinations, all while simply trying to earn an honest living. The memories stung, yet they had taught me valuable lessons about workplace dynamics.

It saddened me that in today's professional world, we still succumb to jealousy and insecurity. Experience has taught me that another's success doesn't diminish our own, yet many still operate as if promotions and achievements are zero-sum games. While I believe in healthy competition, I genuinely celebrate others' opportunities for growth. Unfortunately, each time I've risen professionally, I've lost friendships and collegial bonds. This pattern led me to downplay my education and achievements, especially around female colleagues, fearing they would hold my success against me. For years, I deliberately dimmed my light to avoid making others uncomfortable. Yet, through it all, I've learned that none of us should feel compelled to minimize our achievements. The rare "work BFFs" I've encountered proved that while shining alone can be powerful, our light grows stronger when we illuminate each other's paths.

Entering the dingy parking garage, I quickly adjusted my makeup, choosing subtle gloss over bold lipstick. Thoughts of my children and grateful husband carried me through the elevator ride to an eerily empty reception area. Finding no staff present, I settled into my office, following a desk note's instructions to contact IT for computer setup. Sitting alone in that vast space, I couldn't help channeling Elle Woods from "Legally Blonde," wanting to shout "ME!!!" at achieving the VP position. Yet the moment felt hollow without colleagues to share it. My 54th-floor corner office offered spectacular views, but the absence of my team members cast a shadow over my accomplishment. Their avoidance couldn't stem from personal dislike or feeling threatened. They didn't know me yet. Still, the isolation stung. In the days that followed, some staff members began trickling in, each interaction tinged with coolness. My attempts to learn about the organizational culture met with resistance. When I asked one team member for guidance, she deflected by claiming unfamiliarity with work she had clearly managed for years. I maintained my professional demeanor and was excited to be invited to a meeting that

same afternoon which included all of the VPs from our organization. I was excited to meet them and was hoping they would be more welcoming than my team. However, I encountered varying degrees of reception. While most peers offered surface-level pleasantries, one woman approached with a calculated smile, commenting on my Harvard MBA. "Well, nowadays, it doesn't really matter where you get your MBA from. I guess it comes down to who you know," she remarked, launching into a critique of every MBA holder she knew. As she spoke, my mind drifted to graduation day, that milestone moment when I became the first woman in my family to earn an advanced degree while my brothers followed the traditional path into our family's mechanical business. Rather than engage with her negativity, I excused myself gracefully. Then I met Laura. Her warm eyes and genuine smile offered the first authentic welcome I'd received. Apologizing for her absence on my first day, she explained her mother's illness had kept her at the hospital. "I was so excited to hear you were joining our team," she shared, introducing herself as one of my direct reports. What followed was an honest conversation about our department's dynamics. Laura revealed the underlying resistance: the team felt threatened by my education and experience, questioning why they should accept an outsider's leadership after their years of service. "They'll give you a hard time at first," she warned, "but please don't quit. These women are broken, but they will come around." Her words offered both insight and hope. Over the next six months, I focused not just on my responsibilities but on demonstrating the power of mutual support and guidance. Gradually, the resistance thawed. Within a year, the transformation was visible. I remained with the organization for seven years, accumulating numerous successes while learning from every setback. By my second year, my department ranked first in all performance metrics, an achievement that might have come sooner had we not spent months overcoming initial resistance.

Laura's approach exemplified ideal team dynamics. She viewed my arrival not as a threat but as an opportunity for mutual growth. Her attitude created an environment where both of us could learn and develop. Our collaborative relationship proved that one supportive voice can sustain you through challenging transitions.

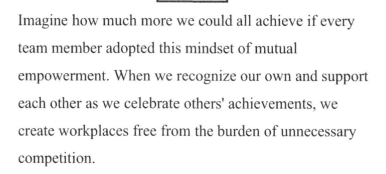

Imagine how much more we could all achieve if every team member adopted this mindset of mutual empowerment. When we recognize our own and support each other as we celebrate others' achievements, we create workplaces free from the burden of unnecessary competition.

Through this journey, I learned that true leadership isn't about dimming your light to make others comfortable; it's about creating an environment where everyone feels empowered to shine. Together, we can build organizations where success isn't a zero-sum game but a collective achievement that lifts us all higher.

Three Essential Takeaways:

1. Transform Resistance Through Understanding

• Look beyond surface behaviors to underlying fears

• Meet defensiveness with compassion

• Build bridges through consistent, authentic leadership

2. Cultivate Collaborative Success

• Create environments where mutual growth thrives

- Celebrate individual and collective achievements

- Transform competition into cooperation

3. Honor Your Authentic Leadership

- Maintain your standards while building connections

- Lead with both confidence and compassion

- Create space for others without diminishing yourself

Remember: True organizational transformation begins with leaders who understand that lasting change comes not from forcing compliance but from nurturing an environment where everyone feels valued, supported, and inspired to contribute their best.

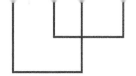

Stress to Strength: Transforming Survival into Success

Aside from my entrepreneur ventures, publishing, and as a HeartMath® Coach for the past decade, I've witnessed the myriad ways stress manifests in people's lives. Through my work as a stress management practitioner, sales professional, speaker and publishing maverick, I've discovered that everyone has different thresholds and baselines, different stories they tell themselves about what causes their stress. What I've learned is particularly crucial because every person has a unique threshold for stress management.

Let me share a personal story that transformed my understanding of stress and thriving. For most of my corporate career through my thirties, I operated in pure survival mode, thinking this was normal. Then came the wake-up call: I found myself in the emergency room with a severe panic /anxiety attack. I had no idea what was happening; I just thought this was how everyone felt, and frankly, this state had been quite normal for me. I had

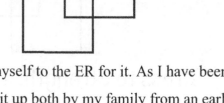

simply not taken myself to the ER for it. As I have been taught to just suck it up both by my family from an early age and by military culture, I was forbidden such displays of weakness. No exaggeration.

The nurse who treated me that day changed my perspective forever. When I demanded a pill so I could return to work, she looked me straight in the eyes and gently laughed. "No," she said, "you have a bigger, more serious problem. This can't be solved with a pill. You need to address your lifestyle and understand why your body is having such severe reactions. Look at you! You can barely stop shaking." Do you know what a panic attack is? she asked. Do you know what PTSD is? My face went blank. I said, what is that? She smiled. She said, "sit down".

This incident forced me to confront the reality that my workaholic tendencies and constant drive to compete and make more and more money weren't sustainable. As a true American capitalist, I had convinced myself this was normal. But our bodies cannot operate under constant duress and stress. I began to look for ways to understand

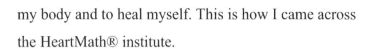

my body and to heal myself. This is how I came across the HeartMath® institute.

In the HeartMath coaching program, we emphasize understanding these individual baselines. As a leader who goes beyond the call of duty, you must know your team members and what they bring to the table, their unique attributes, and how these qualities can benefit both the organization and specific projects. Through carefully designed assessments, I help individuals understand their stress levels and develop personalized strategies for managing them. Of course, I learned about the HeartMath Institute because of my anxiety as I was looking for alternative ways to heal.

The demands of a corporate career for women are intense, as evidenced by countless studies, including recent research from Sheryl Sandberg's Lean In organization. The data is clear: women, particularly minority women like myself, miss out on millions in lifetime earnings and the workload demands are quadrupled compared to non-Latino women. This isn't about complaining; it's about acknowledging reality so we can create positive change. This meant that my stress levels were a result of both outer pressures and internal dialog. My outer pressure just tends to be quadrupled and more damaging than most white women. That's the truth, as data indicates. In all reality, I had no shot at real progress and achievement unless I dealt with my crushing trauma responses, and even then, I'd be way behind most of my peers just by the mere fact of being Latina.

Through my journey from surviving to thriving, I've discovered several essential tools. The most powerful is connection. Research consistently shows that human connections are fundamental to happiness and success. This is why organizations like LeanIn, as mentioned above, have created platforms for women to gather in small groups worldwide, fostering conversations and mutual support.

My personal toolkit has expanded through involvement with organizations like Toastmasters and the National Speakers Association. While only some people need to be public speakers because of the nature of their careers, these communities have helped me maintain connections

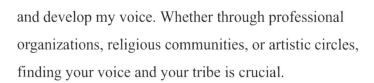

and develop my voice. Whether through professional organizations, religious communities, or artistic circles, finding your voice and your tribe is crucial.

Drawing from my extensive corporate experience from managing T-Mobile stores to becoming a regional director in the telecommunications industry and later in finance operating multi-million-dollar operations in Nevada I've concluded that nothing is more valuable than creating communities and sharing resources. While I've invested over a quarter-million dollars in my professional development, the most impactful growth has often come through free collaborative environments like LeanIN Circles and similar frameworks.

So how does this pertain to transforming stress to strength and surviving into thriving?
My journey from corporate warrior to conscious leader reveals a fundamental truth about success: we cannot sustainably achieve our goals while operating in constant survival mode. My wake-up call came in an emergency room, where a compassionate nurse helped me see that my "normal" state of anxiety and stress was actually a

serious warning signal. As a Latina executive managing multi-million dollar operations, I was facing not just the typical pressures of corporate leadership, but also the quadrupled workload demands that research shows minority women often shoulder. You know they say ignorance is bliss and well to a certain degree it was, until it wasn't. LOL

The transformation began when I stopped viewing stress management as weakness and started seeing it as essential leadership wisdom. Through HeartMath® coaching and deep personal work, I learned that true strength comes not from "sucking it up" or pushing through lessons ingrained by both my family and military background but from understanding and honoring our individual stress thresholds, what I call baselines as a HeartMath® practitioner.

The key lies in acknowledging our reality while refusing to be limited by it. When we understand our stress responses, build supportive networks, and learn to regulate our nervous systems, we don't just survive, we create new possibilities for ourselves and those we lead.

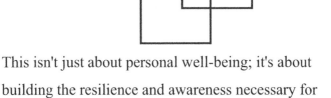

This isn't just about personal well-being; it's about building the resilience and awareness necessary for lasting leadership impact.

For those in C-suites and executive roles, I encourage you to assess your agenda by asking three crucial questions:

1. Is it worth your mental health?
2. Is the money worth the cost to your well-being?
3. Are you truly taking care of the people you love while helping stakeholders maintain profits?

The key difference between surviving and thriving lies in awareness. Women who merely survive often operate unconsciously in a fight-or-flight state, unaware of their stress levels. Those who thrive understand their physiological state before walking into any corporate space. They practice self-regulation and show up authentically, in a state of giving rather than stress.

For those who haven't yet developed this awareness, we must offer grace. The most important thing is to focus on your own growth while planting seeds for others. During my corporate years, I shared transformative books like Darren Hardy's "The Compound Effect," understanding that personal development, like compound interest, grows exponentially over time.

Key Points for Women to Thrive:

1. Develop Stress Awareness: Understand your baseline and learn to regulate your physiological state through tools like HeartMath techniques.

2. Build Meaningful Communities: Whether through Lean In circles, professional organizations, or informal networks, create connections that support your growth.

3. Invest in Continuous Learning: Make personal development a priority, understanding that small, consistent investments in yourself compound over time to create extraordinary results.

Remember: The path from surviving to thriving begins with awareness and is sustained through authentic

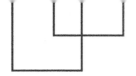

connection and continuous growth. When we show up-regulated and authentic, we create environments where everyone can excel. Your mental and physical well-being aren't luxuries; they're essential requirements for true leadership success.

A Story: Man is Promoted Over Woman

A new workday began when I left my house in the early hours of the morning, and it was still pitch dark outside. I was glad I wore my warm boots lined with wool as I walked in the cold to my car. I had parked outside the night before because I did not want to get stuck another day in my condo's parking garage like I did the day before. I needed to be at work bright and early. We had a new client coming in, and all my blueprints for their ads still needed to get printed. I had been up until 2 a.m. editing the documents because they were not perfect until they finally were.

I sat in my car that morning, thinking about my life and all the challenges. I was driving with the faint sound of the early morning news in the background, lost in my thoughts. I thought about my work and smiled. I loved my job and felt it was time for me to move up to a higher position and continue to learn. Stopped at a traffic light, I noticed that I was the only car on that dark street. Most of the apartment complexes around me had their lights off;

people were still sleeping. Not me. I was on my way to work.

That morning, I realized I had been working so hard that I had not thought about the next steps in my career. I had been doing the same job for the past six years. "It is time!" I thought to myself. I decided it was my turn to speak to my director about my next steps and promotion.

I carefully parked my car in the creepy underground parking lot. Leaving the warm and cozy seat, I started walking toward the tall building. The elevator bell rang, and I was on the 45th floor. I walked over to my desk, quickly set my handbag and coat aside, and started working. I opened the blueprint files again and checked them one more time before printing them out. I pressed print and went to the kitchen to make some coffee before everyone started arriving.

I loved our fully stocked kitchen at work, especially the variety of creamers that changed with each season. It was time for my favorite- pumpkin spice. Unlike coffee shops, I only added two pumps of pumpkin spice syrup, not three. I was proud of my refined taste buds, requiring less sugar to enjoy the flavor. In anticipation of my meeting, I decided to be a little antisocial until after the big pitch and went back to my desk to review some emails and the pitch deck.

There it was: the email I had always dreamed would be about me someday. "We are thrilled to announce the promotion of...." Only it wasn't about me. Shocked, I realized the position had been open without my knowledge. I read the name: "Dennis Burns!" Him again! He had only been in the department for two years, while I had worked at the organization for six. My evaluations always earned the highest ratings. I was labeled the "perfectionist" and the "role model" of the department. My work ethic was unmatched, and my work quality, as some said, was "perfectly perfect."

Yet Dennis was at every big meeting, presenting and getting exposure to leadership that was never offered to me. I had excellent public speaking skills, but when I asked to present, I was told the board generally preferred hearing from other leaders or directors. So why was Dennis selected for those opportunities? It was then I

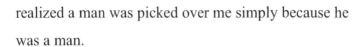

realized a man was picked over me simply because he was a man.

I realized leaders could be weak. All along, I was told I was next in line, but my boss, a woman, did not support or empower me. She said the right things but never delivered. I viewed Julia as a mentor. A couple of months earlier, Julia told me how pleased the marketing firm was with me. Yet, when presented with opportunities to highlight me, she didn't.

I continued to read the email. It was painful to scroll through and realize my promotion was a dream, not a reality. I wouldn't get that promotion at this company, not because I lacked skills, talent, or qualifications, but because my mentor was my roadblock. All the marketing tools and templates were my designs. The company's growth strategies were my ideas. Yet, I was never recognized. So buried in work, I didn't search for opportunities and didn't know the position was posted. I naively thought my boss would approach me directly. She didn't.

Dennis was a great colleague: pleasant, kind, and smart. I was smarter. I had better ideas, always found solutions, and taught others. Dennis didn't. He focused on himself, speaking up about his aspirations, while I focused on perfecting my work. He often praised himself in meetings. I thought his demeanor was fake and assumed others saw through him. I was wrong.

Disheartened, I sat at my desk, wondering why Julia didn't tell me about the opportunity or select me. Dennis spoke up, took action, and made his vision clear. Julia knew my aspirations but didn't advocate for me. I kept my head down, trusting my mentor and loyalty to protect me. They didn't.

Soon after Dennis started his new position, I began applying elsewhere. I quickly became the marketing manager at a competing firm. My career kept moving upward. I now own a marketing firm with 200 employees, one of the largest in the Western U.S. I often wonder why Julia didn't support me. Over time, I realized she didn't have a vision for women in power. Julia was lovely but carried biases she likely didn't recognize.

Today, I am thankful for those experiences. They taught me to recognize biases, especially as women. We must support each other and build more women leaders who lead with compassion, not aggression. Women can lead with their hearts, embracing their innate strength. My most meaningful successes came when I led with compassion.

Key Takeaways for Leaders

1. **Address Unconscious Biases:** Actively recognize and challenge unconscious biases in decision-making. Foster transparency in promotion processes, provide bias training, and implement practices like blind recruitment to ensure equal opportunities for all employees, regardless of gender or background.

2. **Advocate for Talent:** Recognize and champion deserving team members. Ensure opportunities are communicated transparently and advocate for individuals based on merit, not biases. Foster an environment that supports women and underrepresented groups in leadership roles.

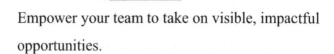

Empower your team to take on visible, impactful opportunities.

3. **Encourage Self-Advocacy:** Create a culture where employees feel safe voicing their aspirations. Offer mentorship that equips team members with the tools to articulate and pursue their career goals confidently.

Legacy Rising: Building the Next Generation

Without vision and purpose, people perish. While this ancient wisdom's original source may be debatable, its truth resonates deeply in our mission to inspire the next generation of women leaders. We must educate ourselves and our children to understand that life extends beyond accumulating material possessions. Our obligation lies in leaving a legacy that transcends monetary wealth, though we should certainly strive to leave our children financially secure. More importantly, we must focus on passing down ethical standards and ideals that will enable future generations to thrive. I've always loved the expression of planting a tree that you know you will never sit under when it can provide shade… or something like that. LOL. This idea of leaving an ethical will of sorts is a cornerstone of my life philosophy. No doubt ambitious.

This understanding was crystallized during my time working with world-class coaches, including John

Maxwell, recognized as the world's leading leadership coach. Through extensive training in personal development, marketing, finance, and public speaking, one truth became abundantly clear: nothing matters more than the legacy we leave for the next generation. While creating a legacy might sound lofty or unattainable, it begins simply with our immediate family. When you can craft an ethical will for your children, you can extend that impact to your community. From community, it expands to city, from city to country, and ultimately to the world. The key is starting small and growing organically.

"The most important thing a man can leave behind is not what he leaves in the pockets of men but what he leaves in their hearts." The deep understanding of this revelation forced me to confront an uncomfortable truth: for years, I had been building solely for myself accumulating accolades, certificates, writing books, and joining prestigious associations, desperate to prove my worth to the world. Through intensive coaching and a lot of soul searching, I realized my intention was simply to impress others. For those of us over 40, there comes a profound realization that much of what we learned until that point requires reevaluation. At 40, I discovered I no longer needed to impress anyone. Instead of pursuing more certifications or reading more books, it was time to implement what I'd learned and create the impactful legacy I'd long discussed, wrote about and yearn to build as part of leaving a dent in the universe. I'm sometimes embarrassed it took me until 40 to realize it wasn't about me. It's always been about building others up and creating value for them. I was 40, for goodness sake; I had proven to myself I could accomplish nearly anything I set my mind to. The goal shifted to contributing meaningfully to others' lives, focusing particularly on inspiring and building a legacy for my two children. In my forties, I finally realized that I wanted my children to learn earlier what took me decades to understand: that no amount of degrees, leadership conferences, or photos with celebrities like Oprah, Tony Robbins, Les Brown, Deepak Chopra, or Wayne Dyer truly matters. (They are really cool, though) What matters is that we leave in people's hearts a sense of love and genuine human connection because they interact with you in a moment in time. Like looking in a mirror (kind of).

While some say touching one soul is enough and that's a humble sentiment humans are capable of impacting communities, nations, and the world. Whether through writing, blogging, poetry, or leveraging new technologies, our potential for positive influence is limitless. For young women leaders specifically, we have a responsibility to present an honest narrative about leadership. Corporate life is messy, and sugar-coating does a disservice to the next generation. Instead, we must prepare them with essential tools, particularly the soft skills that enable meaningful connections and collaboration. The most valuable tool for young women today is learning to be authentic without compromising their standards or conforming to a world designed by and for men. It's crucial they understand that feminine leadership qualities, connection, compassion, and empathy are strengths, not weaknesses. The future belongs to heart-centered leaders that understand this at a soul level.

Legacy Through My Sons' Eyes

One evening after dinner, my older son, who had followed my footsteps into military service as a parachute rigger, called me with an unexpected reflection. "Mom,"

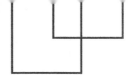

he said, "I found your old leadership books while helping uncle organize the garage. I remember watching you study those for hours when I was little, always chasing the next certification or achievement. But you know what I really remember? The day you stopped trying to prove yourself to everyone and started teaching me about what truly matters."

He shared a memory from his childhood, long before his younger brother was born, when he asked why I had so many pictures with leadership figures on my office wall. Instead of boasting about meeting John Maxwell or being in the same room as presidents, I had sat him down and explained that all those achievements meant nothing compared to the moments we shared together, the values we pass on, the love we give to others. "You taught me that true success isn't about the leadership conferences or who you meet," he continued. "It's about how you make others feel, how you lift them up. I understand that now in my role as a parachute rigger – the precision and care I put into each pack isn't just about the job, it's about the person whose life depends on my work."

Years later, having these same conversations with my younger son, I see how the lessons evolved and deepened.

The legacy of understanding that true leadership comes from the heart has taken root in both my boys, though they learned it in different seasons of our lives. My younger one often says, "Mom, your real trophies aren't on your wall – they're in the stories you share and the people you help. "In these moments, I realize my real legacy isn't in the quarter-million dollars spent on professional development or the prestigious associations I've joined. It's in these two young men, taught in different decades but carrying the same core truth: authentic leadership comes from the heart, true success lies in helping others grow, and our greatest achievements are measured by the lives we touch, not the accolades we collect.

That's the ethical will I hope to leave not just to my sons, but to every young leader finding their way: Start with heart, lead with authenticity, and always plant trees of wisdom whose shade will benefit generations to come.

Three Fundamental Aspects of Legacy:

1. Mentorship and Sponsorship: Take young people under your wing, coach them, and open doors through your connections. Success often depends more on relationships than resumes.

2. *Values Over Accolades:* While prestigious education can open doors, success isn't limited to Ivy League graduates. Focus on building character and capabilities rather than collecting credentials.

3. *Multi-Generational Impact:* Shift the conversation from material wealth to creating lasting change through compassion, honoring our ancestors, respecting our elders, protecting our planet, and acknowledging those who contributed to our success.

In our capitalist society, the importance of legacy transcends simple bullet points. It's about repairing our collective soul and creating positive changes that echo through generations. Honoring those who came before us while building a better future for those who follow may be the most profound contribution we can make.

Let me share how theory transformed into action through the Latinas100™ community, an organization I founded in 2019. What began as a local initiative to leave a legacy has blossomed into a movement spanning 17 countries, demonstrating how one small vision can create a rippling impact across generations.

The core mission of Latinas100™ was simple yet powerful: eliminate barriers to entry in publishing. We've helped hundreds of women, many without traditional means or access to information, publish their stories for the first time. By teaching them the intricacies of the publishing industry and providing free resources, we've empowered voices that might otherwise have gone unheard. The impact has exceeded anything I could have imagined. These women haven't just published, they've created their own clusters of communities across the globe, particularly in Latin America. They support each other at book fairs, collaborate on marketing, and most importantly, build lasting connections that transcend borders and generations.

Perhaps the most profound testament to this legacy comes from two of our writers who have since passed away. Their contributions to our anthology series collections

featuring hundreds of writers in a single volume became their final goodbyes to the world. Had it not been for these publications, their voices might have been lost to history. Instead, their stories live on, touching lives and inspiring others. This experience beautifully illustrates what one person can achieve when focused on creating a lasting impact. As Darren Hardy emphasizes in "The Compound Effect," transformative change starts small but requires consistency and pure intention. You begin with a simple idea, stay committed to your vision, and watch it grow beyond your wildest dreams.

I share this story not to showcase achievement but to inspire possibility. If I could create this impact, so could you. Legacy isn't about grand gestures; it's about consistent, intentional actions that ripple outward from family to community, city to country, and ultimately to the world.

Remember: We're capable of leaving legacies that transcend generations. Whether through writing, teaching, mentoring, or creating communities, each of us has the power to shape the future. *The key lies not in the* *scale of our initial action but in the purity of our intention and the persistence of our effort.*

Our responsibility to the next generation isn't just to show them what's possible, it's to create pathways that make those possibilities accessible. That's the true meaning of legacy, and it's available to anyone brave enough to begin.

A Story of success: at what cost

Choked up. Sad. My heart was beating really fast. So much anxiety. Fear. Hopeless. Scared. These words sum up the price a woman must pay if she is both beautiful and successful in the workplace. She can never really complain about it because that would make her a spoiled, entitled brat! How dare she complain? According to most people, the world caters to beautiful people; therefore, if she is beautiful, she should not complain about anything. This is what society teaches us. Our society also teaches us the definition of beauty. Beauty is defined in magazine ads, social media, commercials, movie lead characters, etc. Yet, if you look around, I mean if you look at each person around you, you can easily find beauty.

I'm at a coffee shop today. I'm looking at this older woman with gray hair who is slightly hunched, yet her beauty is in her smile. Her smile brightens the room. I'm looking at the young woman placing her order at the register. Clearly, she is trying not to be attractive. Her big Doc Martens and baggy pants with the huge, oversized flannel shirt would not categorize her as America's top model. Yet, when you look at her, the innocence in her eyes and the way she carries herself is beautiful. The little Pakistani girl next to me is staring at me. Her eyes have captured me. Every single person in this coffee shop is beautiful to me. Yet because we allow society to define what beauty is to us, we are also victimizing so many women, men, boys and girls. We are victimizing them because while they are categorized as beautiful, our society labels them as just that. And society teaches us that beautiful people are not smart either. And this is why if you see a beautiful woman in the workplace, it is assumed that she is not so smart. And if she speaks like she is smart, that throws everyone off. And so it begins! The retaliation, the defensiveness, and the wrong accusations on people who, first of all, didn't ask to be categorized as beautiful, and second of all, they just want to work and do a good job. Instead, our society victimizes them, and we end up punishing them.

I had a wonderful friend named Katie. She was loving, warm, beautiful, and smart. We had so many laughs together. She had the laugh of an angel and the witty sense of humor of John Stewart. We had conversation after conversation about her ideas at work and how she would improve processes. She was always so excited about the work she did. I would find her to be the first in the office and the last to leave, more often than not. Her boss loved her and praised her for her hard work and dedication to each and every project. She worked with her heart and really came through in her work. She brought millions of dollars worth of revenue to the organization. Yet all our colleagues in the workplace labeled her as not being smart. They said she was sleeping with her boss. They made up rumors to make her seem like she was not smart enough to do the job. What always took me by surprise was that these were always the women in the group who would start the nonsense. No one really took the time to get to know Katie. They judged her, especially the women.

The sad part is that when I would talk to Katie, she didn't really see her outside beauty. She longed to have great, meaningful friendships. Yet she always felt misunderstood. Both women and men painted a picture of her that was not accurate. It did not match up to her. Katie wanted to make a difference at work. She wanted to bring forth a culture of acceptance and diversity in her environment. Instead, she was never given the opportunity. Anytime a promotion would come up, one person or another would make a flimsy excuse why she should not get the promotion and would promote someone less attractive. She had the experience and the education, but no one around her would give her the opportunity. Yes, I agree; our society is designed to cater to those who have been defined as beautiful. Yet, society catering to beautiful people really is skin deep. That means that society caters to the superficial side of beauty. And really, that can only take you so far.

One day after work, Katie and I were working really hard in our offices. The law firm we worked at was a very demanding work environment. We were both paralegals. She had started her job three years before me. There was a vacancy in the firm for an executive paralegal. Katie stopped by my office to say hello and talk a little. We had a lot in common, and our biggest commonality was that we both loved working. She was always three steps ahead of me, though. She knew the laws so much better, and as much as I wanted to have her memory, that would never happen. She let me know that she had applied. She also let me know that she knew I had applied. We both looked up at each other and said, "Well, may the best woman win." We were both so excited. We made plans about what our life would look like after one of us was selected for the job. Katie was amazing. Deep down, I knew I really didn't have a chance against her, but I was ambitious, and she didn't feel threatened by me, so it made the process easier. That evening, we reminisced about the time when I started working at that firm and how she mentored me throughout that entire time. We both had several interviews for the job and were going to hear the results the next morning. We both walked out of the office at around nine PM and wished each other good luck.

At six AM the next day, we both entered the building at the exact same time. We burst into laughter after seeing each other ready to tackle the day with our lucky black suits and white blouses on. I wore my pearls, and she wore her super cool necklace with her name engraved on it. Although I played the part and really wanted the position, deep down, I knew that Katie was more educated, experienced, and so much more qualified than I was. I just went in and prayed for Katie first and then myself. Heads down and working on briefs, we were each called to the Partner's office. This was a firm with only women's leadership. So, I thought they would pick the most qualified candidate. I smiled at Katie as we both walked in different directions of the office. At the west wing, I opened the door to find Marcia wearing her power suit, looked up at me and smiled, as she poured water in two glasses for both of us from a crystal jug.

I knew what was coming. I was just fine with getting a rejection as long as Katie was the one getting the promotion. I stood up straight, widened my shoulders and eyes, took a deep breath, and was ready to shake hands and walk out of the office and let them know that I would apply for a future job. But that did not happen. Marcia let me know that I got the job and that they thought I could bring a lot of great experience to the team. I was shocked! I couldn't understand why they did not pick Katie for this job.

Marcia looked at me, and we smiled. She said, "Congratulations, you deserved this." I asked her about

Katie. She said, "Well, we couldn't really pick her. I mean, look at her." She continued, "We thought that if all the young lawyers and interns would see her, they would surround her desk, and she would never get anything done." My eyes grew wide at hearing this. I could not believe it. Sure, for a second, I felt like chopped liver. However, when I stepped outside and saw Katie crying in her office, I felt sorry for her. I guess society does not cater to beautiful people in a meaningful way. Sure, they may give her a free coffee or an upgrade, but when it really matters, society is actually very brutal to beautiful people. Especially as women, instead of working on ourselves and our self-esteem, we torture other women around us for being smarter, prettier, or better in any way. What's worse is that we find ways to justify our behavior.

Years later, Katie did end up getting a promotion. Yet so many people, including her boss, gave her such a hard time during and after the process. Four months after getting her promotion, I called Katie and asked her how she was doing. She said she loved her job and everything she was learning, yet she felt that the energy around her was toxic. Her direct boss was an older woman who was abrasive with her, mainly because she was jealous of her. Katie's subordinates retaliated against her if they got any chance. Her peers wouldn't really help her and thought that she should figure it out herself.

Looking in from the outside, Katie had it all - beauty, smarts, and a great job! Yet when I asked her how she was doing, she said, "I have it all now, but there is a price to pay the more you climb." When I asked her what that price was, she said, "Choked up. Sad. My heart was beating really fast. So much anxiety. Sadness. Hopeless. Scared."

Lessons learned: Don't judge a book by its cover. Wouldn't it be wonderful if we could not see outer appearances and were judged solely on our performance and our interactions with others? Wouldn't it have been great if Katie's new boss had taken her under her wing, helped her in the new role, and made sure she succeeded? Wouldn't it have been great if Katie's subordinates looked to her with hope and guided her as she learned her new job? Wouldn't so much of the negative vibes that linger in the workplace disappear if people chose to be helpful

instead of hurtful? I imagine we would be a much more productive, positive, and efficient society. Don't you?

Three Key Takeaways:

1. *Foster Supportive Leadership*
- Mentor based on potential, not perception
- Build inclusive team environments
- Address toxic behaviors directly

2. *Challenge Unconscious Bias*
- Recognize that beauty bias works both ways
- Evaluate performance independently of appearance
- Create objective criteria for advancement

3. *Transform Workplace Culture*
- Promote collaboration over competition
- Celebrate diverse forms of success
- Create safe spaces for authentic leadership

Remember: True professional value lies in capability, character, and contribution - not in conforming to or defying society's expectations about appearance and ability.

Final Insights: Dr. Wajhma Massoumi Aboud

Reflective Triumphs: Embracing Authentic Leadership in Corporate America

Reflecting on these interconnected stories, a powerful truth emerges about women's leadership in corporate America. Through the experiences of accomplished professionals facing similar yet distinct challenges, we see a recurring theme: the transformative power of authentic allyship and collaborative leadership.

Each narrative from the new VP balancing motherhood with hostile workplace dynamics, to Monica's journey beyond corporate barriers, to Samantha's triumph over both personal health battles and professional obstacles, to Katie's navigation of beauty bias demonstrates how women often face multiplicative challenges rather than simply additive ones. We're not just dealing with individual biases or isolated instances of competition; we're confronting systemic patterns that require systemic solutions.

The title "Who Does She Think She Is?" captures both the challenge and the solution. This question, often wielded as a weapon against ambitious women, reveals deep-seated assumptions about who "deserves" to lead and how they should do it. Yet through heart-centered leadership, these women transform that very question into a declaration of authentic power. They show us that the path to professional excellence isn't about conforming to traditional leadership models or competing for limited resources - it's about creating new models that embrace both strength and compassion.

The framework of collaborative success emerges not as a nice-to-have, but as a strategic imperative. When women choose to support rather than compete, to mentor rather than undermine, to celebrate rather than resent others' success, we don't just lift individuals - we transform entire organizational cultures. This isn't about merely surviving in hostile environments; it's about creating new environments where all can thrive.

These stories teach us that the heart-centered path to professional excellence requires courage on multiple fronts: the courage to face bias, the courage to support others even when we feel threatened, and the courage to lead authentically even when it costs us. Yet they also show us that when we commit to this path, we create ripple effects that transform not just our own careers but the very landscape of corporate leadership.

The power of collaborative frameworks lies in their ability to create sustainable change. One woman achieving success despite obstacles is admirable; women working together to dismantle those obstacles is revolutionary. This is how we move from asking "Who does she think she is?" to declaring "This is who we are" leaders who understand that true excellence comes not from outcompeting each other, but from creating spaces where all can excel.

Final Insights: Adriana Rosales

Lifting as We Rise:

A New Blueprint for Women's Leadership

As I reflect on the stories within this manuscript, I see a tapestry woven with resilience, ambition, and the hard-earned wisdom of women who dared to dream of a better workplace. Each narrative mirrors a segment of my own path, grappling with the dual challenges of leadership as a woman. They remind me why redefining the roles that women play in corporate culture is vital and why the heart of that redefinition lies in collaboration, not competition.

Collaboration as Power is actual power and is the key to unlocking our full potential as women and as leaders in all corporate spaces.

Growing up in a Latino household taught me the strength of community. Life was about working together, lifting each other, and succeeding as a unit. However, stepping into corporate America was a different world where women were often set against each other and made to feel that success was a finite resource. I've lived this tension and seen how destructive it can be. It's why I believe so profoundly in rewriting this narrative. This book is meant to do just that. To rewrite a narrative that has primarily been written by and for men. This must end, and we must rise to write our own stories and the way we wish to interact with each other while we do business with each other.

The stories of Monica, Samantha, and Katie hit close to home. They remind me of the many times I've had to prove myself over and over again, not just because I was a woman and a Latina but because I was a woman who dared to lead authentically. They remind me of the moments I've had to summon courage in the face of unkindness or push through the loneliness of being a leader in a room full of hostility. But they also remind me of the women who showed me grace, who saw my potential, and who helped me rise.

Feminine Leadership as a Strength
Through years of leadership experience, I've come to understand that the qualities often labeled as "feminine

"compassion, emotional intelligence, and collaboration are not just beneficial; they're essential. They bring balance to environments dominated by competition and individualism. The stories in this book illustrate how these traits transform teams, foster trust, and unlock innovation. They also show what happens when women deny these strengths out of fear or societal pressure.

For me, leadership has always been about more than strategy or results; it's about people. It's about creating environments where everyone feels valued, where their potential is nurtured, and where they leave each day better than when they arrived. That kind of leadership takes courage, but it also takes an unwavering commitment to authenticity and connection.

The Legacy We Build Together

If there's one lesson I've learned that echoes through these stories, it's this: **Leadership is about legacy**. It's about what we leave behind for the next generation of women. For too long, women have been taught to fit into molds that don't honor their strengths. It's time we break those molds. We need to show our daughters, our

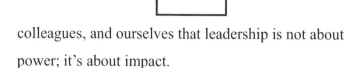

colleagues, and ourselves that leadership is not about power; it's about impact.

When I think of the legacy I want to leave, I imagine a world where women are not just surviving in corporate spaces but thriving. A world where they are supported by other women, where their successes are celebrated, not resented, and where they are free to lead with their full, authentic selves.

A Call to Action

To the women reading this: Know that your voice matters. Your leadership matters. And most importantly, your support of other women matters. Together, we can rewrite the narrative. We can build a culture where collaboration and integrity define success, where competition becomes inspiration, and where every woman has the opportunity to lead, thrive, and create her own legacy.

Afterword

In this exceptional book, Adriana Rosales and Dr. Aboud have intricately captured the essence of women's leadership, authenticity, and organizational transformation. Through compelling personal narratives and evidence-based insights, they illuminate the often-overlooked challenges women encounter in corporate environments while offering practical solutions for meaningful change.

What resonates deeply with my research on authentic harmony is how these stories highlight the vital interplay between feminine and masculine energies in leadership. By exploring life stories through the lens of the Ruler, Philosopher, Magician, or Sovereign archetypes, each chapter reveals how women navigate these energies to create their unique leadership signatures.

The authors' focus on stress management, heart-centered leadership, and legacy-building aligns seamlessly with what I have observed over decades of research. True organizational transformation emerges when the masculine drive for results is balanced with the feminine capacity for connection. The authors' emphasis on authentic leadership, particularly through narratives about overcoming workplace bias, fostering team dynamics, and embracing personal growth, reinforces the idea that sustainable success lies in integration rather than separation.

This book is both a reflection of current challenges and a guide to a brighter future. It illuminates a path forward where authentic feminine power is recognized as an essential ingredient in organizational success. The authors' vision of creating cultures where women can thrive without dimming their light offers not only hope but also actionable guidance for the next generation of leaders.

I hope that readers will embrace these insights to foster workplaces where both feminine and masculine energies are equally valued, where heart-centered leadership becomes the standard, and where authenticity is celebrated. The transformation envisioned here—where competition gives way to collaboration, stress becomes a source of strength, and legacy transcends individual achievement—is not only possible but essential for the future of business and leadership.

An essential handbook for wise leaders, male and female alike!

With gratitude,
Dr. Pauline Crawford
Author of The Power of Authentic Harmony
Gender Dynamics Intelligence Expert & Leadership Consultant

About the Authors

Dr. Wajhma M. Aboud stands as a distinguished leader in finance and administration, wielding over 18 years of experience in controlling, planning, and budgeting within multifaceted academic healthcare environments. Currently, she serves as the Director of Association Management Services at the American Academy of Ophthalmology, where her visionary leadership continues to shape the future of healthcare. Previously, at Stanford University, Dr. Aboud garnered acclaim as a transformative force, skillfully bridging the gap between senior leaders and medical professionals to foster collaborative excellence.

Her academic journey reflects a relentless pursuit of knowledge and innovation. Dr. Aboud holds an Executive Master of Business Administration (MBA) from Washington State University and a Doctor of Medicine (MD) from Universidad Iberoamérica in the Dominican Republic. Additionally, she earned a Bachelor of Arts in Psychology with a minor in Chemistry from the University of San Diego, embodying a unique blend of scientific insight and humanistic understanding. Throughout her career, Dr. Aboud has exemplified a steadfast commitment to strategic planning, financial

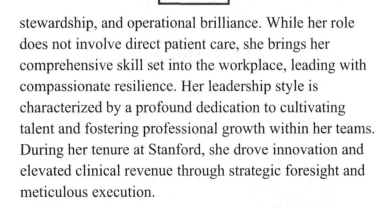

stewardship, and operational brilliance. While her role does not involve direct patient care, she brings her comprehensive skill set into the workplace, leading with compassionate resilience. Her leadership style is characterized by a profound dedication to cultivating talent and fostering professional growth within her teams. During her tenure at Stanford, she drove innovation and elevated clinical revenue through strategic foresight and meticulous execution.

Dr. Aboud's multilingual fluency enhances her capacity for cultural competence and effective communication, enabling her to connect with diverse stakeholders in healthcare. She is resolutely committed to bridging disparities in healthcare access and quality through inclusive leadership and pioneering management strategies. Her contributions extend beyond impressive metrics; they reflect a deep-seated commitment to nurturing environments where healthcare professionals can thrive and patients receive exceptional care.

As a leader, mentor, and advocate for excellence, Dr. Wajhma M. Aboud's impact resonates profoundly within the field of academic healthcare. Her journey embodies the intersection of medicine and administration, illustrating that visionary leadership can transform the lives of both providers and patients. Through her enduring dedication and compassionate approach, Dr. Aboud inspires a new generation of healthcare leaders, championing the belief that exemplary management is paramount to delivering quality care.

Adriana Rosales is a distinguished author, publisher, and former expert panelist and writer of the Forbes Coaches Council, whose diverse career began in the United States Air Force as a Command Post Specialist in Space Command. Based in the United States, she stands as the innovative founder of the LATINAS100™ community and Rosales Mavericks Publishing Studio (RMPStudio™), where she dedicates herself to empowering aspiring authors, with a particular focus on elevating marginalized voices.

Her multifaceted career spans military service, telecommunications, and finance. Her educational journey includes San Jose State University, and she has served as an adjunct professor at the College of Southern Nevada. As a certified HeartMath® Coach and John Maxwell International Speaker, she brings a wealth of experience to her role as a mentor and leader.

Central to Adriana's philosophy are the pillars of Trust, Courage, Compassion, and Service, principles she first embraced during her military career and later showcased in her book "Corporate Code," where she guides corporate executives through her proprietary *TCCS method*. This ethos not only underpins her coaching, training, and mentoring but also shapes her approach to the world of publishing. As an accomplished author with over 100 published works under the RMPStudio™ imprint, Adriana is a guiding force for emerging writers navigating the intricacies of publication.

At RMPStudio™, Adriana and her team are dedicated to supporting first-time authors. They provide an array of services, from editing and design to marketing and distribution, ensuring that each story reaches its audience with impact and integrity. Her expertise and experience make her an invaluable mentor to those eager to share their narratives. Her upcoming book **"The Book Coach Whisper"** maps out a writer's journey from start to finish, drawing from Adriana's own publishing experience. She will also be launching her memoir in 2026, ***"Satellite Love: Letters to Myself"***

For those aspiring to make their literary mark, Adriana is more than a successful publisher and author. Drawing from her military background and subsequent achievements, she is an inspirational figure in storytelling and leadership, committed to helping individuals express their unique experiences and insights through the written word.

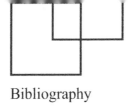

Bibliography

JournalAntiTrust. (n.d.). *JournalAntiTrust*. Retrieved from https://academic.oup.com/antitrust/article/1/1/162/274807?login=false

KevinKruse. (n.d.). *EmployeeEngagement2.0*. Retrieved from https://www.gyda.co/tools-and-resources/book-recommendation-employee-engagement-2-0-by-kevin-kruse

LeanIN. (n.d.). *Women in the Workplace*. Retrieved from Women in the Workplace: chrome-extension://efaidnbmnnnibpcajpcglclefindmkaj/https://cdn-static.leanin.org/women-in-the-workplace/2024-pdf

MedTRADE. (n.d.). *MED*. Retrieved from MedTrade: https://medtrade.com/news/legislative-advocacy/survive-improvise-collaborate-and-prevail/

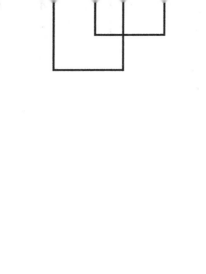

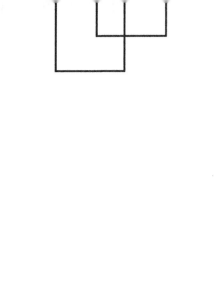

Made in the USA
Middletown, DE
07 February 2025